Bill's

THE COOKBOOK

BILL COLLISON **AND** SHERIDAN McCOID

with
LOVELY
PHOTOS BY
DAN
JONES

BILL's

THE COOKBOOK

COOK
EAT
SMILE

BILL COLLISON *AND* SHERIDAN McCOID

SALT · YARD
BOOK Co.

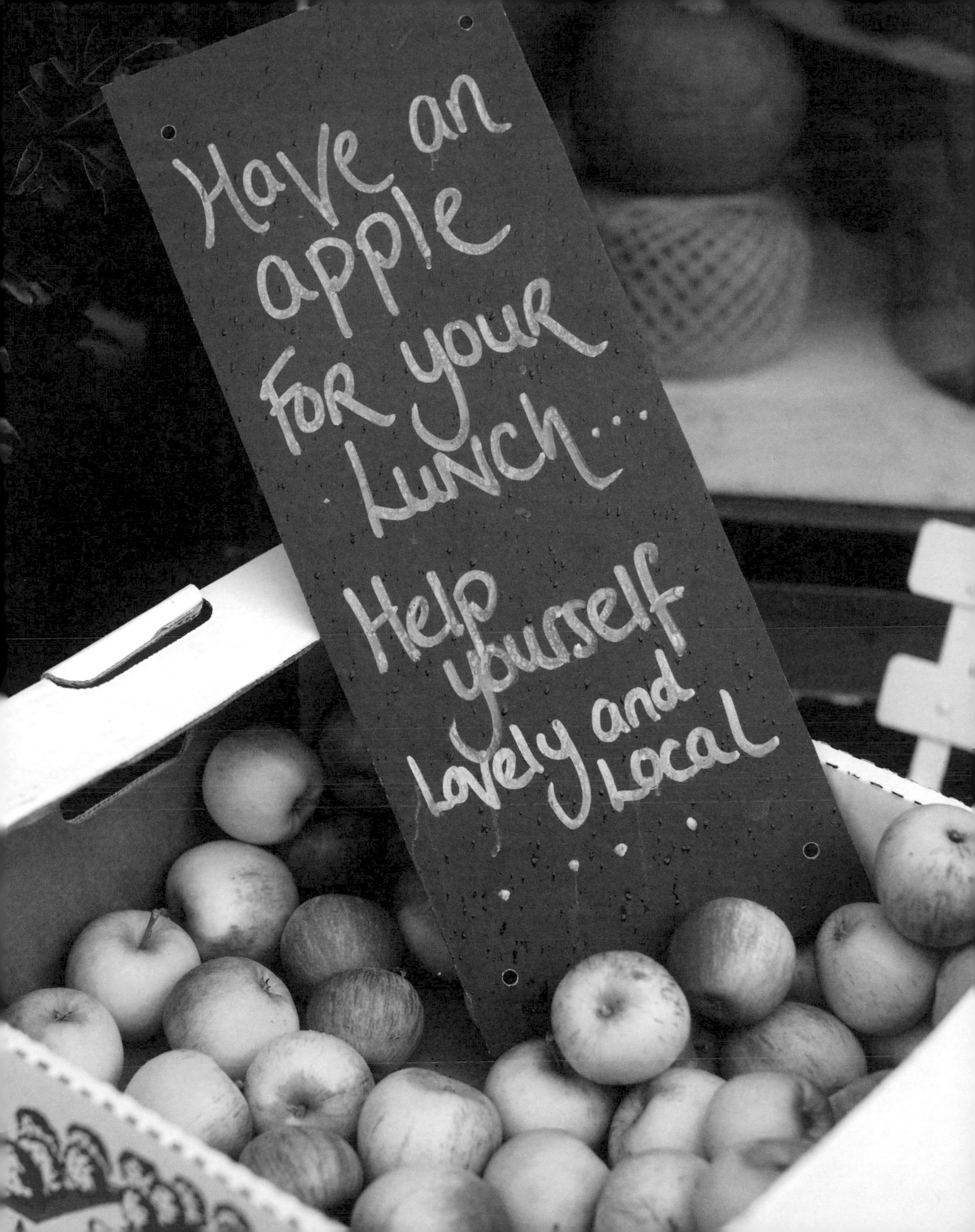
Have an apple for your Lunch...
Help yourself
Lovely and Local

Bill's

CONTENTS

A sandwich in the sun

We opened the first Bill's Café in 2001 and really none of us could have imagined how successful it would become. We'd talked about it for long enough and we hoped that people would like it, but what we couldn't have guessed was that people would love it, that they would go out of their way to come to the café and then go and tell all their friends about it. It was fantastic.

Then we won some awards, including the *Observer Food Monthly* Best Newcomer in 2006, so more people got to hear about us and before we could blink, our relatively small café in a relatively small town near the south coast became a bit of a sensation.

What had started as some ideas and a lot of hard work, had become a real, live and kicking, rustle and bustle place for people to meet for coffee or lunch or tea and to buy some good, local produce to take home to cook for supper.

We filled baskets with seasonal fruit and vegetables, and shelves from floor to ceiling with Bill's jams and chutneys. We baked, cooked and served deliciously different food, hung skeins of raffia from the ceiling, stacked towers of produce and hired lively, enthusiastic staff to look after our customers. We wanted Bill's to be somewhere that really celebrated food and was welcoming to everyone. We wanted new customers to stop in their tracks to take everything in as they came through the door, and for regulars to feel like it was the next best thing to home.

We set out to make a place that was colourful and exuberant, with dishes that were really tasty but that also made you smile, that put everyday and unusual seasonal ingredients together and gave everyone lots of ideas to take home with them. We put fruit on our pizzas, we added roots, sprouts and leaves that people had never seen before to salads, we made cakes that looked so extraordinary that customers stopped to take pictures before they ate them. All of this, we've tried to capture in this book.

How did I end up here? My dad owned a nursery just outside Lewes, and we grew up, my brother and I, working pretty hard and learning about how the seasons work, how the weather works, what growing stuff involves, how great it feels when all the hard work pays off and things do actually grow and you pluck them off a tree and bite in to them or bring them inside and cook them.

When I was 22, my dad, fed up with what I was doing with my life, showed me a small shed down a lane off the High Street and said I could make of it what I would. It was mine, to get me started. The only thing I knew about was fruit and veg and so I opened a tiny little greengrocer's shop, which became a bigger greengrocer's right on the High Street a few years later. I knew what to do and not only that, I loved it. I was at home.

And then one night in October 2000 a flood swept through the town destroying hundreds of properties, including my shop and my house, on its way. The day after the flood, we set up a makeshift stall on the High Street. I needed to keep trading if I could and we stayed like that for months, right through the winter, as the town slowly crept back to normality.

In 2001 we opened Bill's Produce Store and Café, and that was it — the beginning.

A good few years ago, we made a decision to stock mostly produce that was in season. At times it's been pretty challenging but we, and our customers, have got in to a rhythm and really look forward to and welcome the first of the new produce with open arms. Rhubarb! What took you so long? Strawberries! How good to see you at last! The Champions were born.

So, with the Champions as our guide, from the first of spring's new potatoes all the way through to midwinter jewels like oranges and pomegranates, the Bill's cookbook is a tour of the seasons and all their glories. We've packed it with recipes and ideas, celebrating the best of our favourite fruit and vegetables as they dip in and out of season, and using them for everything from fresh juices to pizzas, and from breakfasts to birthday cakes.

As well as a celebration of the Champions, what to do with them and what other ingredients they like to share a plate with, this book drops in for tea with many of the year's festivities, throwing together a no-bake cake for Mother's Day and the mother of all mezze spreads at Christmastime.

Eating should be a simple pleasure, whether it's a noisy affair with friends and family gathered round the table or just you and a sandwich in the sun. So have fun — explore new foods, experiment with new flavours and get out there and cook something to make you smile.

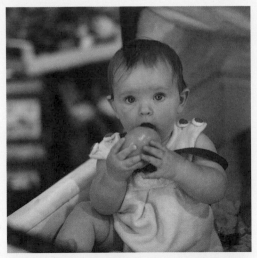

Spring

GOOD TIMES
AHEAD

Spring can be a bit of a tease. So desperate are we to wave goodbye to winter that, at the slightest hint of warmer days, we're out there freezing in shorts, trying to have picnics and rushing to the garden centre.

And nobody is more desperate than us gardeners. I've usually been planning what I'm going to do in the garden since the last days of summer and by February I'm champing at the bit to get stuck in with my spade. I've pored over seed catalogues, I've ordered, they've been delivered, I've read the back of the packets and seeded those that I can. Hurry up! Let's get going!

But while we may be ready to throw open the windows and let the show begin, the good earth's bounty is still tucked up in bed and, like a teenager, will not be roused before it's good and ready.

And yet… it may feel like the dog-end of winter, but the sap is rising, roots are stretching and there's a whole lot of growing going on out of sight, and so, with buds and shoots to help us keep the faith, we wait. And while we wait, we get busy making plans for Easter, temporarily and optimistically forgetting that it is likely to be one of those horizontal-rain-lashing-at-the-window days, and we dream instead of something insane like lunch in the garden.

And then, just when we're beginning to think that we're stuck in a vortex that is forever winter, with daffodils been and gone, like buses (teenage buses) everything decides to roll out of bed at the same time and suddenly we've gone from wintry pulses to asparagus with Jersey Royals and bright green broad beans and a jug of creamy hollandaise alongside, and it's all aboard and off we go and welcome to spring.

Bill's

SPRING CHAMPIONS

Good things definitely come to those who wait and when spring's fresh, new, colourful produce arrives, we can all heave a sigh of relief as the seasonal calendar starts rolling.

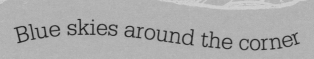

Blue skies around the corner

Asparagus

Slender stems of goodness

Nutritionally one of the most well-balanced vegetables, full of fibre, high in folic acid, packed with vitamins and minerals, what's not to like about this delicate-flavoured stem?

Well, to start with, it is quite expensive. Then, already strange-looking, it doesn't help to know that, left in the ground, spears develop in to ferns and, at the height of the season, can grow 20cm in 24 hours. And yet I am not the only one who couldn't care less if they only recently arrived from Planet Zorg, because when the first of the season's bundles of asparagus finally make their way in to the shops, customers can't get enough of them. And, because the season is so short — maybe a couple of months, a little more if we're lucky — I have two pieces of advice: eat it while you can and don't overcook it.

Steam it, grill it, roast it, layer it in to a pastry case for a simple tart or blend it in to soup if it's past its squeaky, snappable best. Dip the long green stems in to softly boiled eggs or warm hollandaise as often as possible, and weave them in to a hat to wear about town. Do all of these and more while the asparagus season lasts.

Warm asparagus, poached egg and Parmesan salad

The easiest way to cook asparagus is to dry-fry or griddle it – quickly, delicately – enhancing and adding to the flavour and texture of the spears with some crisp charring. This dish has a really fast turnaround time if you poach, warm and griddle simultaneously. Serve with some good crusty bread for mopping up every last drop of golden yolk.

SERVES 4

Lightly oil a frying pan or griddle and get it good and hot before laying the asparagus spears flat on the heated surface. Depending on the size of your pan, you may have to do this in batches, but each batch should only take a couple of minutes. Turn the spears or roll them over now and then to ensure they cook through without burning – although a little charring and blackening is good.

While the asparagus is griddling, poach the eggs for 2-3 minutes in simmering salted water with a dash of vinegar. Warm the hollandaise sauce, if you are using it (see recipe on page 26), and get four plates ready by putting a generous handful or two of salad leaves on each.

Divide the crispy asparagus spears between the plates, spreading them over the leaves, and drizzle with olive oil. Drain the poached eggs using a slotted spoon and carefully balance one on each heap of asparagus and leaves. Spoon some hollandaise over the top if you like, then finish with a good handful of fresh Parmesan shavings, some sea salt and a grind or two of black pepper. Scatter some chive flowers over the top for a springtime flourish.

olive oil, for griddling
  and drizzling
300g asparagus, trimmed
4 medium eggs
4 tbsp hollandaise sauce
  (optional)
plenty of mixed salad leaves
Parmesan, for shavings
chive flowers, to garnish

Spear tips

Eat asparagus as soon as possible, certainly within a day or two, as it deteriorates quickly. If you're not eating it straight away, store the stems in the fridge in a vase or jar of water.

Most of us tend to throw away more than we need to, lopping off a good few centimetres from the bottom, whereas you can quite often take a peeler to that end, get rid of the woody exterior and eat the rest.

If you're steaming asparagus, try to keep as much as possible away from the water. Cut the ends off (if that's what you're going to do) after cooking as opposed to before, to give a little more lift in the pan. A bit of an angle is OK; just keep the tips out of the water. A sharp knife to the stem will let you know when they're cooked.

Hollandaise is the traditional accompaniment – with good reason. Make it yourself (see recipe on page 26) or buy a decent ready-made sauce. From here you're just a step away from a very classy dish that involves toasted sourdough or muffins topped with grilled asparagus, smoked salmon, poached egg, hollandaise and Parmesan shavings.

Bill's spring champion

New potatoes
Making good chefs of us all

New potatoes herald spring and allow us to finally slam shut the winter cookbooks, as they suit everything that's lighter and fresher — all the foods we've been longing to tuck in to.

The loose-skinned new potatoes from Majorca arrive first, followed by Italian Spunta, Cyprus new potatoes (my favourite for baking) and the Cornish Earlies.

And then in roll the Jersey Royals. They let the others do the warm-up and then regally swan in, taking their place at the top table with a price tag that makes you laugh and a season that's so short you wonder why they bothered. Labour-intensive little blighters for the growers, but they're worth every penny for that sweet, earthy taste, and so the answer, as far as cost is concerned, is to make them the centrepiece of a meal rather than an accompaniment.

Baked, roasted or boiled, thrown in a salad, topped with a poached egg or grilled halloumi, paired with spinach or ham, sprinkled with bacon and Parmesan and black pepper... I could go on, but do I really need to?

Well, OK. You could, for example, boil them, drain and then stir in some fried pancetta and onion. Add a poached egg and a good grinding of black pepper. All you then need are some fresh green leaves to complete the picture. Or you can make them go further by mixing them up with plenty of other spring vegetables.

First and simplest: throw a handful of mint sprigs in a serving dish. Tip freshly boiled or steamed new potatoes on top. Add some good butter, black pepper and a sprinkle of salt and stir to melt the butter through.

Roasted new potatoes get very excited about hollandaise sauce (see recipe on page 26). Serve the two together, a bowl of each, both warm, to dip in to before a meal. Add a glass of wine and good company. If you don't have hollandaise, sweet chilli dipping sauce is also good.

Boil the potatoes till just cooked, tip in to a baking dish and then squish the potatoes with the back of a fork. Add some bacon if you like, cut in small slices, or some pancetta. Slivers of garlic, chopped rosemary and/or thyme sprigs and some paprika – sweet or smoked – will all bring something to the party, but really the potatoes are good on their own. Drizzle a good slug of olive oil across the top and sprinkle with sea salt. Bake in a hot oven (around 200°C/180°C fan/gas mark 6) for 20-30 minutes, until crisp and golden. This is good topped with a poached egg, and with a peppery watercress salad on the side.

Using the smallest potatoes, roll them in sea salt and then roast in a hot oven (200°C/180°C fan/gas mark 6). This should take around 30 minutes. Once they're cooked and while they're still warm, cut a little cross in to the top, pinch them to open up and fill with humous (see recipe on page 279) or cream cheese or broad bean mash and mint (recipe on page 49) or guacamole (recipe on page 282).

For an instant spoon-over dressing for warm new potatoes, mix a good slug of olive oil with some yoghurt, crème fraîche or mayonnaise. To mix the flavours up you can add a spoonful of horseradish sauce or mint jelly or wholegrain mustard. And to take things even further, you could stir in a handful of rocket, fresh baby spinach or beetroot leaves, or some finely shredded kale or chard. Add a good spritz of lime or lemon juice to finish, if you have some, to give it a lift.

Broad beans

Emerald isles

I love the way broad beans float like little emerald isles on top of soups. I love the bright greenness of the peeled beans, their delicate flavour, their versatility and the fact that they are one of the first crops that deliver for us growers.

You don't get a lot from a bag of pods, a batch often yielding only a small bowlful, but all it means is that you have to savour each little gem. And if skinning the individual beans, slipping each one out of its coat, seems like more trouble than it's worth, all I can say is — it isn't. Maybe with the very earlies you can get away with eating them with their skins on, but after that it's definitely time to blanch them, then, once they're cool enough to handle, grab the colander and head for a warm spot in the garden for a spate of peeling. All worth it to get to that soft-textured, sweet-flavoured, brightly coloured kernel.

Pan-fried broad beans, new potatoes and chorizo

A quick and easy mid-week supper. You can add all sorts to the base ingredients of broad beans and new potatoes. Here, we've used chorizo, which will bring a spicy kick to proceedings. But instead you could add some dry-fried halloumi or some crumbled feta right at the finish, and a poached egg will often hit the spot at the end of a long day.

SERVES 4

Wash the potatoes and cut them in chunky halves, quarters or thirds. Put them in a pan of boiling salted water and simmer for 10 minutes, or until just tender. Remove from the heat and drain.

Melt the butter in a large frying pan over a medium heat and add the cooked potatoes with plenty of freshly ground black pepper, stirring now and again to stop them from burning and sticking. When the potatoes are golden, add the broad beans and continue to stir occasionally.

While the broad beans are cooking, fry the chorizo in another pan till golden brown, then stir it and its cooking juices in with the potatoes and beans. Serve in a large bowl, with the basil leaves scattered over the top.

900g new potatoes
40g butter
1.2kg broad beans (weight in pods), podded, blanched and peeled
2 small chorizo sausages (approx. 200g), chopped in 1-2cm chunks
a small handful of basil leaves

To blanch broad beans, drop the podded beans in a saucepan of boiling salted water and cook for 3 minutes. Then transfer them to a bowl of ice water to refresh them. You should then be able to peel the skins off easily.

Watercress

Lean, green, health-giving machine

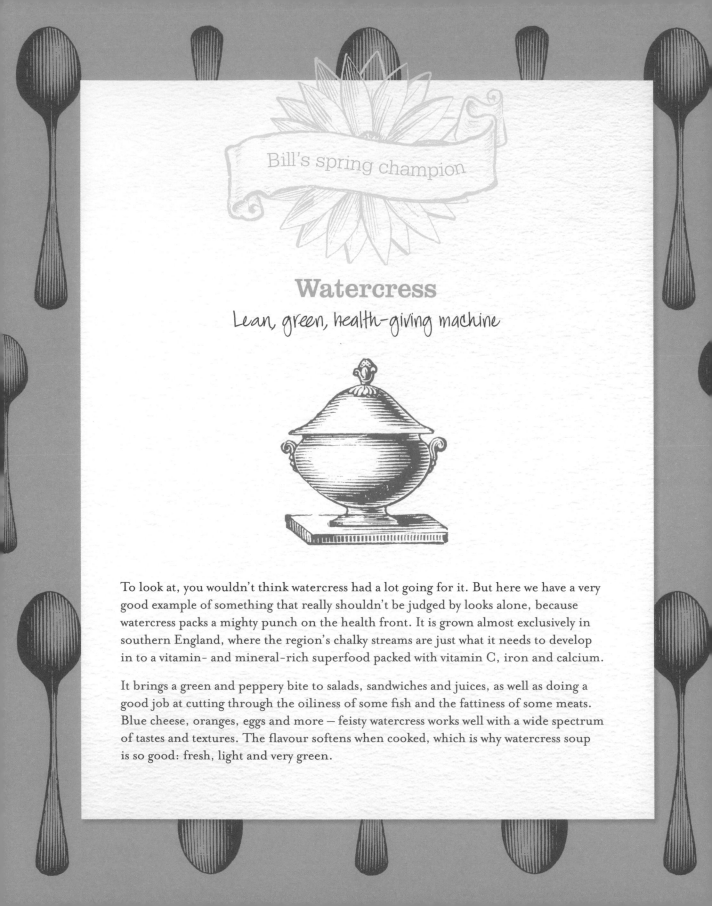

To look at, you wouldn't think watercress had a lot going for it. But here we have a very good example of something that really shouldn't be judged by looks alone, because watercress packs a mighty punch on the health front. It is grown almost exclusively in southern England, where the region's chalky streams are just what it needs to develop in to a vitamin- and mineral-rich superfood packed with vitamin C, iron and calcium.

It brings a green and peppery bite to salads, sandwiches and juices, as well as doing a good job at cutting through the oiliness of some fish and the fattiness of some meats. Blue cheese, oranges, eggs and more — feisty watercress works well with a wide spectrum of tastes and textures. The flavour softens when cooked, which is why watercress soup is so good: fresh, light and very green.

Watercress and potato soup

SERVES 8

Cook the onions, celery and potatoes gently in the oil in a large pan for 15-20 minutes. Setting a few sprigs aside for garnishing, add the rest of the watercress and cook gently for a further 5 minutes.

Add the stock and simmer for 10 minutes then, making sure the soup is cool enough to blend without scalding, liquidize everything until very smooth. Bring back to serving temperature in the pan, stir in the honey and season with salt and freshly ground black pepper, and a grating of nutmeg if you like it.

Serve each bowl of soup with a spoonful of crème fraîche and a watercress sprig.

2 onions, diced
1 stick of celery, diced
600g new potatoes,
 washed and cut in chunks
1 tbsp olive oil
3 bunches of watercress
 (approx. 250g), washed
1.25 litre hot vegetable stock
1 tsp honey
nutmeg (optional)
crème fraîche, for serving

Bill's spring champion

Eggs
Sunny side up

If you have space enough for a shed or a climbing frame in your garden, then you have space for a hen house and run, and really, I can't think of any better addition to a garden than a couple of hens. Having said that, they will scritch and scratch all over the place when you let them out, so best not if your garden is a place of ordered beauty. But if it's a place of barely controlled beauty and you can develop clever ways of keeping them away from precious plants, hens will bring you a huge amount of pleasure, especially when you step outside in the morning to collect their eggs.

And never more so than in the spring. Partly because the garden's beginning to stretch its legs and I can check its progress as I nip across to let the girls out in the morning, but also because with no artificial light to keep the hens laying plentifully through the winter, it's been slim pickings for a while. Naturally, seasonally, Easterly and happily, this is the time for eggs, as chickens wake up to enjoy the longer days, shake out those feathers and get laying.

I'm a big fan of eggs: scrambled, poached, boiled, fried — they all have their moments. Sometimes, when you're feeling a bit world-weary, there's nothing like a simple boiled egg and a stack of soldiers to make you realise things aren't quite so bad after all. Equally, when it feels like something is missing from a dish, you'll often find the improvement you're looking for is a poached egg — it has that knack of whooping many a savoury dish in to something more complete.

Fresh, local, free-range and, if possible, organic: the better the eggs you can afford, the more you'll notice the difference. And then you're off, with eggs the starting point for so many good things, from custards and sauces to soufflés, cakes and quiches. That one scrawny, twitchy, feathery old bird might be the beginning of something as light and beautiful as a meringue or as pretty and fresh as lemon curd is truly miraculous.

Bill's hollandaise sauce

Buttery, lemony, rich and light all at the same time, hollandaise is a delicious and luxurious sauce, made with expensive ingredients. Which is why it's so upsetting when it all goes pear-shaped or, to be precise, curdles.

I reckon as many attempts at hollandaise sauce end up being poured down the kitchen sink as make it to the table, with crestfallen and harried cooks fuming about the wasted ingredients, throwing down their aprons and abandoning their *Masterchef* dreams. But, if you take it slowly and are careful not to overheat at any stage, there should be a happy ending.

Bill's hollandaise is made with crème fraîche instead of olive oil. Purists may sneer, but it is less costly than olive oil and has all the taste and smoothness we're looking for.

MAKES ROUGHLY 250ML

Put the egg yolks, lemon juice and vinegar in a food processor and whizz for 5 minutes.

Shortly before the end of the 5 minutes, put the butter in a small pan and melt it, making sure it just begins to sizzle but not burn. Pour the melted butter in to the food processor, keeping blitzing all the while until fully blended.

Pour the mixture back in the small pan, stir in the crème fraîche and put on to heat for 30 seconds, whisking continuously. Remove from the heat and ideally serve immediately.

Or you can keep it warm for a while in a covered heatproof bowl over very gently simmering water or in a Thermos flask until you're ready to serve up.

* For what to do with the egg whites, have a look at the chocolate swirl meringues on page 28 or the lemon meringue roulade on page 70.

4 egg yolks*
the juice of half a lemon
2 tbsp white wine vinegar
125g salted butter
2 tbsp crème fraîche

Eggs Benedict

The combination of flavours and textures in Eggs Benedict is almost too good to be true. Ham or bacon is traditional, but you can substitute smoked salmon to make Eggs Royale or spinach to make Eggs Florentine. Whichever you choose, the two ingredients that really ought to get a room are the hollandaise and the poached egg. Clearly, they were made for each other.

The true origins of Eggs Benedict are lost in time, but there are so many claims and counter-claims about who first created it — mostly centred around New York — that its glamour precedes it. This note of transatlantic sophistication is probably what makes it so popular with weekend brunchers in our cafés. That, and the fact that it's a mighty fine way to eat eggs on toast.

SERVES 4

Assuming you have everything ready, as well as some coffee brewing and fresh orange juice poured, you can assemble quickly by dividing the muffins or toast between four plates. Top each muffin half or slice of toast with a piece of ham, a poached egg and a generous helping of hollandaise. A good grind of black pepper and a copy of the *Wall Street Journal* complete the piece.

4 muffins, split and
   toasted, or 8 slices of
   fresh white toast, buttered
8 slices of honey-roast ham
8 eggs, poached
250ml hollandaise sauce,
   warm

Chocolate swirl meringues

That you can turn a bowl of gloopy, viscous liquid in to something as glorious as a meringue — and with very little effort — is a marvel. Which is why making them brazen and bouffant, rippling them with colour and piling them high, is so befitting. Save dainty for another time: today we party.

You can make these meringues to use up the egg whites left over after making hollandaise sauce — or you can make hollandaise with any yolks left over from making these meringues: it obviously works both ways. Alternatively you could use the spare yolks to make lemon curd (page 66) or a couple of batches of Shrewsbury biscuits (page 66). Or both: have gifts, will come visiting.

MAKES 12

Preheat the oven to 150°C/130°C fan/gas mark 2 and line a large baking tray with baking parchment.

Heat the chocolate in a bowl over a pan of simmering water until melted. Remove from the heat and leave to cool.

Put the egg whites in a large mixing bowl and whisk until stiff peaks form. Add the sugar, one tablespoon at a time, whisking continuously, until all the sugar has been incorporated and the mixture is very stiff and glossy. Drizzle the cooled melted chocolate over the meringue and use a metal spoon to fold it gently through to create a marbled effect with bold chocolate streaks running through the mix.

Carefully place spoonfuls of meringue in 12 large dollops on the baking tray, making billowing peaks on each one with the back of the spoon.

Put the tray in the oven and cook the meringues for 30 minutes. Turn the oven off and leave them to cool and dry in the oven overnight.

To serve, pile haphazardly on a large plate or decorative dish and dust with a little cocoa powder.

100g dark chocolate, roughly chopped or broken
3 large egg whites
150g caster sugar
cocoa powder, to serve

Rhubarb

Pretty in pink

Just when we think we are never going to see any home-grown produce again, in come these bright, fresh, pink, tart, sweet stems with which we can start to shake things up a bit in the kitchen: crumbles, pies, jams, smoothies and — wait for it — hot chocolate with rhubarb purée can all now sit happily on the menu. Ours and yours.

The idea of forced rhubarb, those slender pale pink stems that arrive first, is all a bit strange. Did you know that the rhubarb is picked by candlelight? And originally grown in the Rhubarb Triangle? The farms are in a triangle formed by Leeds, Bradford and Wakefield in West Yorkshire, where once upon a time almost the world's entire crop of forced rhubarb was grown (and where there's still an annual Rhubarb Festival). The crop is harvested by candlelight because it's grown in complete darkness and any amount of light would spoil the pale pink colour of the stems. Imagine that — creeping round those sheds in the gloom and hearing the stems squeaking and creaking as they grow…

The forced rhubarb season is short and should be prized. It's all over by the end of March, when the outdoor crop is usually ready for harvesting, so get in there while you can with those delicate stems. Try serving rhubarb and orange compote instead of apple sauce with roast pork or alongside mackerel, or warm on a scoop of good vanilla ice cream.

Rhubarb is one of those versatile foods that can sit with flavours right across the spectrum. It's a vegetable that masquerades as fruit and as such is happy to swing both ways — you can serve it with meat and fish, or tucked in with almonds, vanilla and chocolate. Mostly though, it starts to get boisterous at the mention of butter, sugar and flour and, as with all great relationships, if it ain't broke, why bother fixing it? The arrival of rhubarb in the shops should ring one bell: rhubarb crumble.

Bill's rhubarb crumble

Rhubarb crumble is one of those dishes that is perfect just as it is. However, at the risk of gilding the lily, I recommend that you also try rhubarb and strawberry crumble, when the early Spanish strawberries are in the shops: the pink and red of the fruits, the blending of their two distinctive flavours, the buttery crumble… what better pudding to see off the last of the cold weather and revive us with a hint of tastes to come?

SERVES 4–6

Preheat the oven to 180°C/160°C fan/gas mark 4 and lightly butter a 23 x 33cm ovenproof dish.

Stir the chopped rhubarb with the sugar, finely grated orange zest and ginger in a large bowl, and then spread it out on a baking tray. Bake in the oven for 10 minutes or so until soft.

Rub the flour, butter and brown sugar together in a large bowl until the mixture resembles breadcrumbs. Add the seeds, hazelnuts and oats and mix together, before stirring in the melted butter.

Place the rhubarb* in an ovenproof dish, sprinkle it with the orange juice, spoon the crumble mix on top to cover and return to the oven to bake for 45 minutes. The top should be golden brown and the juices bubbling up round the edges of the crumble.

900g rhubarb*,
  cut in 3cm lengths
200g caster sugar
the zest and juice of
  1 large orange
1 tsp ground ginger
200g plain flour
75g butter, cut in cubes
150g brown sugar
1 tbsp sunflower seeds
1 tbsp pumpkin seeds
1 tbsp chopped hazelnuts
25g porridge oats
25g melted butter

There are two schools of thought when it comes to what to serve with a crumble: custard or vanilla ice cream. Do you go for the softening, melting quality of ice cream or the high comfort-food score of custard? It's a difficult call.

* You could, if you like, add a couple of extra sticks and a sprinkle more sugar when you're oven-baking the rhubarb. Then just set the additional cooked rhubarb to one side before you assemble your crumble. That way you'll have spare rhubarb cooked and ready to use in the following smoothies.

Rhubarb and banana smoothie

Although there are fewer fresh fruits to choose from than in summer, spring is a very smoothie time of year. Everyone is in the mood for a taste of something fruity and light, especially on warmer days. This one is easily the most popular smoothie in our cafés. You need some baked rhubarb for this, so why not bake an extra couple of sticks when you prepare the crumble on page 33.

MAKES 2 TALL GLASSES

Put the rhubarb, honey or syrup, banana, yoghurt and milk in a blender. Whizz it up until smooth and then taste for sweetness. Add some more honey or syrup if you think that's what's needed, and a splash of vanilla extract if you fancy it.

Pour the smoothie in to glasses and decorate with fruit, flowers and abandon.

2 sticks of rhubarb, cooked
  and cooled
1 tbsp honey or golden syrup
1 banana, roughly chopped
140g plain yoghurt
100ml milk
vanilla extract (optional)

Big breakfast smoothie

To turn the rhubarb and banana smoothie in to something more substantial, you can add a good tablespoon of granola or muesli per person to the blender. See our granola recipe on page 102 or use a good-quality ready-made mix. You can also add semi-dried apricots or prunes, some nuts and, for extra flavour, some cinnamon or nutmeg. Play around with it and see what you get – it's a good breakfast or mid-afternoon snack in a glass.

What started out as hot chocolate…

Once upon a time there were two people messing around in a kitchen. There was some hot chocolate, there was some rhubarb. Tall glasses and straws were to hand. Knowing smiles were exchanged and, without much time passing, a star was born.

I am not suggesting that anyone goes to the trouble or would even consider roasting just one stick of rhubarb, which is about the amount you need for two mugs of this hot chocolate. But, say you decided to make the rhubarb crumble on page 33, which involves roasting quite a lot of rhubarb in the oven, and say, having read this, you think you too might like to discover the joys of rhubarb and chocolate in a glass. Then simply throw another stick or two of rhubarb and bit more sugar in to the roasting tray, and we have ourselves an opportunity.

First of all, the cooked rhubarb needs to be puréed. Make the hot chocolate as you would normally, gently stir in the purée and pour the mixture in to two mugs. It's likely that some swirly cream is called for at this stage and some chocolate flakes. Pierce the creamy topping with a straw or long spoon and prepare to luxuriate. It's subtle – mostly chocolatey, but with that ripple of rhubarb running through it.

Of course, there's nothing to stop you trying the same with a ripple of fresh raspberry or strawberry purée in the summer, when berries are plentiful.

OR…

For a cold version that involves – I should warn you – ice cream and more chocolate, prepare the rhubarb purée and hot chocolate as before, then allow them both to cool. Scoop vanilla ice cream in to a tall glass and pour in the cooled rhubarb and the chocolate. Crumble chocolate flakes over the top. A very good quick pudding.

OR…

Smash up some ginger nuts or chocolate Hobnobs and sprinkle those on top of the ice cream before adding the chocolate and rhubarb. An even better good quick pudding, though the pay-off could well be an hour or two's running around on a football pitch or similar.

Spring salads

Spring is a funny one when it comes to salads, because although it all sounds very promising and full of fresh and new ingredients, the truth is we still have to wait quite some time for any fresh produce action. The solution — and there's always a solution in the kitchen — is to keep injecting new energy in to store cupboard ingredients and then, when the spring produce finally arrives, cruelly dump the old for the new without looking back.

Broad bean, mint, feta and watercress salad

A quick and simple salad using the new season's broad beans, watercress and mint. You can eat it just as it is for a light meal, serve it as a side salad with fish or chicken, or add to it with some quinoa, couscous or new potatoes.

Don't worry too much about quantities – it's the mix of flavours and textures you're looking for – but a half-kilo bag of fresh broad beans (weight including pods) and 100g or so of feta should make enough for a side salad for four people.

Mix some podded, cooked and peeled broad beans together with a handful of torn fresh mint leaves and the crumbled feta in a bowl. Place a generous layer of watercress in a salad dish and arrange the minty bean and feta mix on top. Drizzle a generous slug of olive oil along with the juice of half a lemon, and season with a sprinkle of salt and a grind or two of fresh black pepper.

To blanch broad beans, drop the podded beans in a saucepan of boiling salted water and cook for 3 minutes. Then transfer them to a bowl of ice water to refresh them. You should then be able to peel the skins off easily.

Bill's Israeli couscous salad

Pearl-like Israeli couscous is so named because it is very popular in Israel, where it is known as ptitim. It resembles the tiny grains we are familiar with, but the texture is quite different — smooth rather than gritty — and, although it is made from wheat, it's toasted and has a unique nutty flavour. It can be used in place of normal couscous, pasta or rice in any main course or side dish. This salad is a Bill's classic and we often serve it alongside other salads or as part of a mezze spread.

SERVES 4–6

Bring a large pan of water to the boil. Add the turmeric and couscous, then simmer for 20 minutes. Drain well and, while still hot, stir in the vinegar and lemon juice. Cover and leave to cool.

While you're getting the griddle pan good and hot, trim any tough ends from the asparagus, then coat the spears in 1 tablespoon of olive oil. Griddle for 5-10 minutes until crispy.

Stir the pesto and the remaining olive oil together in a jug, season with salt and freshly ground black pepper and pour this dressing over the couscous. Mix in the kidney beans, spinach and olives. To serve, place the mixture in a wide, shallow dish and top with the griddled asparagus.

You can sprinkle some roughly chopped parsley across the top and/or a couple of tablespoons of crunchy munchy seeds if you like (see recipe below).

1 tsp turmeric
250g Israeli couscous
50ml white wine vinegar
the juice of 2 lemons
125g asparagus
3 tbsp olive oil
2 tbsp pesto
1 x 400g tin of kidney beans, drained and rinsed
200g fresh spinach leaves
275g large stoned olives
a handful of parsley, to garnish (optional)
mixed seeds, for topping (optional)

Crunchy munchy seeds

Toasted seeds are a good topping for all sorts of dishes. You can sprinkle them liberally across salads, pasta, steamed vegetables, baked potatoes, rice, cheese on toast, pizza and more. It's good to have a jar made up so they are to hand for regular sprinkling. You can use just one type of seed or a mixture: half and half pumpkin and sunflower is a particularly good mix.

Preheat the oven to 160°C/140°C fan/gas mark 3.

Spread the seeds thinly and evenly on a baking tray and put in the oven for 5 minutes, keeping an eye on them in case they start to burn. Give them a stir to turn them after a couple of minutes. Remove from the oven and sprinkle liberally with light soy sauce. Return to the oven for a further 5 minutes, but carry on keeping an eye as they'll burn in a moment.

Leave to cool completely before storing in an airtight jar.

Bill's butter bean salad with halloumi

Another Bill's classic, a versatile salad that you can serve with any number of other dishes. In the cafés, we use El Navarrico beans for their flavour and softness. They're butter beans, but better. They come in 600g jars, which is why the starting point for this recipe is 600g of beans. If you can get them (we sell them in our stores), do try them; otherwise use tinned butter beans, or you can always use 300g of dried ones soaked for a few hours and then cooked, if you prefer.

SERVES 6–8

Bring a large pan of water to the boil. Add the butter beans and turmeric, bring back to the boil and then immediately drain and leave to cool. We do this in the cafés and it's worth doing at home, to add the sunshine yellow of the turmeric to the beans. Mix in the kidney beans.

Simmer the passata in a medium pan. Dry-fry the spices in a small frying pan for 2 minutes, then add them to the passata. Remove from the heat and add the lemon juice, sweet chilli sauce and sesame seeds. Allow to cool.

Cut the halloumi in ½cm-wide slices and dry-fry each side until golden.

Mix the beans in to the tomato mixture, season well with salt and freshly ground black pepper and transfer to a serving dish before topping with the warm halloumi and some fresh coriander to garnish.

600g cooked butter beans, drained and rinsed
½ tsp turmeric
300g tinned kidney beans, drained and rinsed
400g passata
½ tsp paprika
1 tsp ground cinnamon
½ tsp ground cumin
1 tsp ground coriander
the juice of 1 lemon
2 tbsp sweet chilli sauce
1 tbsp toasted sesame seeds
2 x 250g packs halloumi
a good handful of fresh coriander, roughly chopped

Keeping it simple

Bread

On the one hand, you have recipes, ingredients, methods and planning, and on the other, you have a few simple elements that come together to make a perfect meal. Some ingredients can pretty much just do it by themselves, like bread. A decent loaf, a few other well-chosen accompaniments depending on the season, and you're off.

What constitutes a decent loaf in my book may not be the same for you. For some, it's a baguette – crisp on the outside, light and chewy inside. For others, it's a hardcore wholemeal, dense with seeds. For me, it's a crusty, chewy sourdough.

From that starting point of a well-made loaf, things just get better: a soft-boiled egg, some good cheese, a jar of chutney, an apple, a bag of ripe tomatoes, sea salt, some very good olive oil – the only preparation is the gathering together of everything in one place and, on a good day, a sunny spot to eat it in.

Do you make your own bread? If you do, you're one step ahead in many a direction, from the simple pleasure of lifting the loaves out of the oven and on to a cooling rack, to the deliciousness of a just-made loaf. Many people are intimidated by the idea of breadmaking, but I would say it's easier to get right than a cake. Start with a simple recipe and before too long you'll be impressing everyone.

At Bill's, we're lucky to have a great local baker like David at Flint Owl Bakery, supplying fresh crusty bread every day. The right bread has always played a major supporting role to many of our dishes. Our soup is served with a doughy, oily focaccia, the mezze is accompanied by a mugful of spire-shaped, crisply toasted sourdough, and savoury fillings are stuffed in to chewy, floury ciabatta. From soldiers Jenga-d in a pile ready for dipping in a boiled egg to curranty tea cakes, toasted and slathered with butter, we aim to please.

Toast, with some bling

Clearly, using bread as the basis for a meal or snack isn't a new idea. Since the first loaf, the first unleavened flatbread, we've been topping it with other foods, from cheese and salad to chunks of meat, chutneys and sauces. We could call these open sandwiches, we could call them toast with something on top. But why would we do that when we can use the word bruschetta? How often do we get to say something Italian and cosmopolitan and so full of promise?

And then, because they sound so continental, we step up to the mark with the toppings. You can't call it bruschetta and then just put pieces of cheese and tomato on top. You have to get fancy. My top tip is to pack in the flavour early on, almost always with a quick rub of garlic across the toasted bread, and then, for added emphasis, whack it up at the end too, with a drizzle of chilli sauce or balsamic vinegar, a spritz of lemon juice or a sprinkle of sea salt.

Each of the following toppings will generously cover four large slices of sourdough or other rustic toast.

Chickpeas with tahini and chilli

If you're cooking the chickpeas from scratch, follow the instructions on page 279. As this topping recipe only makes a small quantity, it's probably easiest to use half a tin of chickpeas, or alternatively make double the quantity of topping — what you don't use now will keep in a covered bowl in the fridge for a couple of days.

Set a couple of spoonfuls of chickpeas and a few bits of chilli to one side to use as garnish. Using a fork, roughly crush the rest of the chickpeas and chilli together with the tahini, lemon juice and olive oil in a bowl. Don't worry about getting the mixture too smooth — we're looking for a good rustic texture here.

Pile the chickpea mash on toasted bread and drizzle with a little extra olive oil and some sweet chilli sauce. Garnish with the whole chickpeas, the reserved chilli and the coriander sprigs and sprinkle with sea salt.

200g chickpeas, cooked
1 fresh red chilli, deseeded
  and finely chopped
2 tbsp tahini
the juice of 2 lemons
4 tbsp olive oil, plus extra
  for drizzling
sweet chilli sauce, for drizzling
a few sprigs of fresh
  coriander, to garnish

Baby tomatoes and olives

Cook the tomatoes one of two ways. Either fry them with the onion in olive oil over a moderate heat until the tomatoes are wilting and crushable — a good 10-15 minutes. Or if you prefer, you can roast them — drizzle with olive oil, and roast for 20 minutes at 200°C/180°C fan/gas mark 6.

When they're cooked, add the vinegar to the tomatoes and onion and season with salt and freshly ground black pepper.

Rub the peeled garlic clove over one side of the slices of toast, then divide the tomato mixture between them. Top with the chopped olives and garnish with purple amaranth or basil leaves before drizzling with a little olive oil to finish.

200g cherry or small plum tomatoes
half a red onion, sliced (optional)
2 tbsp olive oil, plus extra for drizzling
2 tbsp sherry vinegar
I garlic clove
30g olives such as Kalamata, stoned and roughly chopped
purple amaranth or purple basil leaves, to garnish

Butter bean and chorizo with yoghurt and basil

Use the El Navarrico beans available at Bill's for top flavour and texture, otherwise use a good quality brand of tinned beans or dried beans soaked and cooked by you (you'll need roughly 100g of dried beans to yield 200g cooked).

SERVES 6–8

In a large frying pan over a medium heat, fry the chorizo in a tiny drop of oil to get it started. When it's looking golden, after about 5 minutes, add the butter beans and the roughly torn basil and fry everything together for another minute, breaking up some of the butter beans a little with a fork.

Spoon the mixture on toasted bread, and top with a dollop of yoghurt, a pinch of smoked paprika, a few basil leaves and a drizzle of olive oil.

If you want something fancier and you have a small piece of cucumber, you can make the yoghurt in to a raita topping. Peel and deseed the cucumber, chop it finely and mix it in to the yoghurt. Spoon the raita over the butter bean topping, invert a few basil leaves on the top of each bruschetta and drizzle the olive oil across, aiming for some to sit in the leaves.

200–225g chorizo sausage,
 peeled and crumbled
olive oil, for frying and drizzling
200g butter beans, cooked
a small handful of fresh
 basil leaves, roughly torn,
 plus extra to garnish
4 tbsp yoghurt
a pinch of smoked paprika,
 to garnish

Broad bean mash and mint

This mash is also good with grilled halloumi or mozzarella instead of feta cheese, and you could add a few halved baby tomatoes if you fancy it.

Tip the beans in a bowl with the mint, olive oil and lemon juice, season with salt and freshly ground black pepper and then roughly crush with a fork.

Spread the mash on toasted bread — you can rub the toast with a garlic clove first if you like. Then top with the feta, pine nuts, nigella seeds (if using) and extra mint leaves. Drizzle with olive oil and sprinkle with a few dill fronds, if you have some, and a little sea salt to finish.

500g broad beans
  (weight in pods), podded,
  blanched and peeled
3 sprigs of fresh mint, torn
  plus extra leaves to garnish
2 tbsp olive oil, plus extra
  for drizzling
2 tbsp lemon juice
100g feta cheese,
  roughly crumbled
a handful of toasted pine nuts
nigella seeds (optional)
dill fronds, to garnish

To blanch broad beans, drop the podded beans in a saucepan of boiling salted water and cook for 3 minutes. Then transfer them to a bowl of ice water to refresh them. You should then be able to peel the skins off easily.

6

A treat for everyone

Pizza

As far as instant gratification is concerned, different foods hit the spot on different occasions. But I would say that nothing does it quite like a pizza. From waiting impatiently for the local pizzeria to do its best, all the way through to delivering your own Saturday evening creation to the table, a pizza ticks all the boxes. And for everyone, too. From toddlers to grannies, nobody turns their nose up at a slice of pizza.

Good things come to those with a plate

When we first started Bill's, we decided to go completely off-message with our pizza toppings, and the more our customers loved the delicious but unconventional combinations of ingredients, the more we played around. So, with complete confidence I say to you — experiment. Walnuts, hazelnuts, grapes, roasted pear or apple, figs, goat's cheese, cranberries, peas, pomegranate seeds — all good. You don't always need a tomato sauce, but you do always need a spread of something, so try pesto or chutney, a cheese sauce or something of your own invention. And then pile on the toppings — the palate (and palette) is all yours.

But you do need an excellent base. The toppings need to be good, but the base needs to be better. Drum roll, then, for my colleague Marcus, who insisted that if a pizza dough recipe was going in this book, it would be his. He's been a chef, he works in the food industry, he grew up in Italy, for heaven's sake. So, take it away, Marcus.

Pizza base

These quantities will make four large (roughly 30cm diameter) pizzas. If you don't want to make this many, the remaining dough can be used to make dough balls or turned in to focaccia loaves (see page 57).

The very fine Italian 00 flour gives a more authentic pizza dough and most good supermarkets and many delicatessens stock it. If you can't find it, a good hard bread flour will do the job. Semolina flour helps the dough to stay crisp for longer, but if you can't get hold of any you can use fine polenta instead.

You can either make the dough by hand or use a dough hook in a food processor. On this occasion, I'll assume you are making it by hand. Place the flours, yeast and salt in a large bowl. Lightly combine and then add the water, honey and olive oil and bring everything together to form a rough ball of dough. Take it out of the bowl and knead on a floured surface. The dough shouldn't be too sticky. If it is, add a tablespoon of 00 flour at a time until it is smooth and springy.

500g Italian 00 flour
75g semolina flour
7g dried yeast
2 tsp Maldon sea salt
300ml tepid water
2 tsp runny honey
2 tbsp extra virgin olive oil

Wipe a slug of olive oil around the inside of the bowl, place the dough back in it and cover with a damp tea towel. Leave it to prove for an hour or until it has doubled in size.

Knock back the dough on a floured surface and divide in quarters. Knead in to four smooth balls. Place these on a baking tray sprinkled with semolina flour or polenta, cover with the damp tea towel again and leave to one side while you make the toppings.

When you have all your pizza toppings assembled and ready to go, preheat the oven and roll each ball out on a floured surface until you have four pizza bases, each roughly 30cm across. Slide the bases on to lightly oiled baking trays. Now you're ready to pile on the toppings. The following recipes will each cover one 30cm pizza base.

Asparagus and broad bean, with rocket and broad bean pesto

Pretty classy, you have to admit. A flavourful twist on a classic pesto *and* asparagus on one pizza. And prosciutto and mozzarella. What a good dish. What a full-on sample of good Italian flavours and ideas.

To get the necessary 175g of cooked broad beans required for this recipe, you will need around 550g of fresh broad beans (weight including pods) to pod, blanch and peel before you start.

Preheat the oven to 200°C/180°C fan/gas mark 6.

Pick out and discard any of the tougher rocket stems, and roughly chop the rest. Mix together with the other pesto ingredients, either with a pestle and mortar or with a few quick blasts in the blender. Season with salt and freshly ground black pepper.

Spread half the pesto and half the ricotta across the pizza base and top with half the Parmesan. Bake the pizza in the oven for about 10 minutes.

While the base is cooking, lightly coat the asparagus and rosemary sprigs in olive oil, place them on a baking tray and roast in the oven for about 5 minutes until crisp, taking care not to burn them.

Remove the pizza and the roasted asparagus and rosemary from the oven. Spread the pizza with the rest of the pesto, ricotta and Parmesan. Dot with the mozzarella, broad beans and pine nuts, criss-cross the prosciutto and lastly top with the asparagus and rosemary. Whack the pizza back in the oven for a final 5-minute blast.

To serve, drizzle with olive oil, add a sprinkle of sea salt, and a bottle of chilled Bill's beer alongside.

FOR THE PESTO
50g rocket
75g cooked broad beans
20g pine nuts, toasted
2 tbsp olive oil
the juice of half a lemon

FOR THE PIZZA TOPPING
4 tbsp ricotta
40g Parmesan, grated
4 asparagus spears
2 sprigs of fresh rosemary
olive oil for roasting
  and drizzling
2 x 125g balls of buffalo
  mozzarella, torn in pieces
100g cooked broad beans
a handful of toasted
  pine nuts
2 slices of prosciutto

To blanch broad beans, drop the podded beans in a saucepan of boiling salted water and cook for 3 minutes. Then transfer them to a bowl of ice water to refresh them. You should then be able to peel the skins off easily.

Smoked mackerel, bacon, field mushroom and spinach

A good and unusual breakfast pizza. Or, as most of us are unlikely to make a pizza at that time of day, very good as a leftover eaten for breakfast. The nutmeg sits brilliantly with the spinach, the mushrooms *and* the fish. Use a good ready-made tomato sauce or see recipe on page 85. You can substitute mascarpone cheese or yoghurt for the crème fraîche if you prefer.

Preheat the oven to 200°C/180°C fan/gas mark 6.

Firsst spread the pesto and then the tomato sauce over the pizza base, but don't blend them together. Layer on the spinach, mozzarella, bacon and mushrooms. Scatter the mackerel across the top and drizzle with olive oil. Bake till the base is golden and the top is bubbling – about 20 minutes.

To serve, dab the mackerel with the horseradish sauce, spoon on the crème fraîche, grate some nutmeg over the top and scatter the pizza with the torn basil leaves.

2 tbsp pesto
3 tbsp tomato sauce
100g baby spinach leaves
2 x 125g balls of buffalo
  mozzarella, torn in pieces
4 rashers of streaky bacon,
  grilled and cut small
2 field mushrooms,
  thinly sliced
1 smoked mackerel fillet,
  flaked
1 tbsp olive oil

TO FINISH
2 tsp horseradish sauce
1 tbsp crème fraîche
nutmeg, for grating
a handful of fresh basil
  leaves, torn

Mixed vegetables and honey

No quantities here, more of a suggestion for how you can build a great pizza, starting with a rich tomato sauce, then adding whatever you have around, what's in season or just what takes your fancy.

Preheat the oven to 200°C/180°C fan/gas mark 6.

Place purple spouting broccoli, cubed butternut squash, red onion quarters, chunky slices of red pepper and courgette on a baking tray. Add some garlic cloves, still in their skins, and a good splash of olive oil, then, using your hands, mix together to make sure everything is well coated in the oil. Roast until the vegetables are cooked through – about 20-25 minutes.

Spread a layer of tomato sauce on the pizza base (for the tomato sauce, see the recipe on page 85 or use a good ready-made brand). Grate an even sprinkling of Parmesan across the top. Scatter with the roasted vegetables, squeezing the garlic out of their skins, then dot generously with goat's cheese, feta or blue cheese. Bake for 10 minutes or until the pizza base is golden brown and some of the vegetables are beginning to blacken.

When you take the pizza out of the oven, drizzle with a spoonful of runny honey and scatter with fresh herbs, such as marjoram and oregano, before serving.

Dough balls and focaccia

If you're not going to make all four pizzas and you want to make dough balls or focaccia with a quarter or half of the dough mix, shape as appropriate and prove again for up to 1 hour. Dough balls need to be baked for about 10 minutes, while a focaccia loaf made with a quarter of the dough will take 15-20 minutes, both in a hot oven (200°C/180°C fan/gas mark 6). For an authentic touch, dent the focaccia loaf dough with the pads of your fingers and drizzle with olive oil, sea salt and some chopped rosemary leaves before it goes in the oven.

We love you, Mum

A special menu for Mother's Day tea

There are all sorts of mothers. Some expect a big fuss on Mother's Day and others would rather be digging in the garden and carrying on as if it's just an everyday sort of Sunday. But all of them will stop for tea. It could be just that: a pot of tea and a plate of biscuits. If she hasn't had to make it, that will be nice. But why stop at nice? This is Mother's Day, and it's Mum we're talking about!

Here, then, is a tea fit for purpose — little pastries, dainty cakes and then, just when she thinks it's all over, an eye-watering mish-mash of a cake that could only have been made by the children.

Goat's cheese
and red pepper tartlets

• • •

Little Lamingtons

• • •

Iced berry cake

• • •

Tea
Fresh mint, Rose, Earl Grey

Goat's cheese and red pepper tartlets

These are very easy, almost just an assembly job. The children can help or even do the whole thing depending on how old they are. You can make these with onion marmalade, basil or tomato pesto — each is good with goat's cheese — and you can either roast the peppers yourself or use some from a jar; just make sure to drain the oil from them thoroughly.

You will need a 5cm pastry cutter and two 12-hole bun tins — or cook these in two batches if you only have one tin.

MAKES 24

Preheat the oven to 180°C/160°C fan/gas mark 4.

Cut 24 discs of pastry and place them in two 12-hole bun tins. Lightly press down a scant teaspoon of onion marmalade or pesto in each base, cover with a few pieces of pepper and then top with a slice of goat's cheese. Sprinkle with paprika and place the trays in the oven for 15 minutes, or until the pastry and cheese are golden.

Serve warm or cold, with rocket (if using) scattered across the top.

If you prefer, you could make this as one large rectangular tart, spreading the onion marmalade or pesto across the base (but not right up to the edge as you need to leave some room for the pastry to puff up). Arrange the other ingredients across the top, then bake in the oven — slightly hotter than for individual tarts (200°C/180°C fan/gas mark 6) for 30-35 minutes — and then cut in squares to serve.

375g pre-rolled puff pastry
   (1 sheet approx. 35 x 23cm)
half a 340g jar of onion
   marmalade or
   100g good-quality pesto
2 roasted red peppers,
   thinly sliced
300g goat's cheese
   (2 logs, each sliced in 12 discs)
1 tsp smoked sweet paprika,
   for dusting
a handful of rocket (optional)

Little Lamingtons

In their native Australia, Lamingtons are most commonly wrapped in chocolate. And you can do that if you like, but we coat ours in raspberry jam: sponge dipped in jam, rolled in coconut and topped with a strawberry or raspberry. We stack them on trays on the counter and, before you can say 'G'day', they're gone.

They're usually quite substantial but, as befitting afternoon tea, we're aiming for dainty morsels here. When the Australian rugby team comes to tea, you can go twice as big. In fact, as a matter of national pride, you'll have to, or they'll think we're just a bunch of big girl's blouses.

Lamingtons feature here because they're fun — if a bit messy — to make. And they look good and suit a special tea.

Preheat the oven to 180°C/160°C fan/gas mark 4 and lightly butter and line a 23 x 30cm cake tin with baking parchment.

Cream the butter, sugar and vanilla extract together. Gradually add the beaten eggs, and continue beating to make sure they're well incorporated, adding a tablespoon of flour if the mixture begins to curdle. Sift the flour and baking powder together and fold in to the mixture. Pour it in the tin and bake for 35 minutes, until the top is golden and springs back to the touch. Remove from the oven and allow to rest in the tin for 10 minutes before turning out to cool on a wire rack.

When it is completely cool, cut the sponge in squares. You should aim to get 30-40 little square cakes.

Melt the jam over a low heat until it's runny; if there are pieces of fruit, sieve it to make it smooth. (The kids will need a grown-up to supervise while the jam is hot). Put the coconut in a bowl and then get ready for the fun part: place the coconut next to the jam saucepan, which is next to the cake squares.

Stab a fork in a square of cake and hold it over the runny jam. Spoon jam all over the cake till it's well coated and, once it has stopped dripping, move across to the coconut and spoon that over the jammy cake, liberally covering the sponge. Place it back down on the wire rack, best side up. Continue like this with all the squares of cake. Honestly, it's not as messy as it sounds.

Place each little Lamington in a paper case and, for a final flourish, stick a fresh strawberry or raspberry on top with a dab of melted white chocolate.

250g butter, softened
250g caster sugar
1 tsp vanilla extract
5 eggs, beaten
250g plain flour
1 tsp baking powder
250g raspberry or
  strawberry jam
200g desiccated coconut
small punnet of strawberries
  (halved) or raspberries,
  to decorate
50g white chocolate

Iced berry cake

An all-singing, whooped-up, somewhat over-the-top, photo-opportunity cake that requires no cooking at all and can be assembled (because it is essentially an assembly job) by a five-year-old, which is, after all, the point: that it has been, at least in some small way, prepared by the children.

You can use any good shop-bought cake — maybe a Victoria sponge or a lemon drizzle cake. Here, we've used a simple sponge cake that started out with jam in the middle and a dusting of icing sugar on top. Just make sure it's a cake that isn't iced or decorated, because that's where the kids come in.

Smaller children may need a hand with some of this, but older ones can probably manage the whole lot. Let imaginations run riot with the decorations — use whatever the kids think is required. And yes, this could well mean we're talking dog's dinner, but it's all in the spirit of the day, so bite your tongue on tasteful and go with the creative flow. If you're supervising, all you should need to do is melt the chocolate... and manage the mayhem.

Whip the cream until it is thick and softly peaked. Melt the chocolate in a heatproof bowl over a pan of simmering water. Remove the berries from the freezer.

Sit the cake on a plate. Slather the cream across the top, layer on the berries — and put some between the layers if it happens to be a jam-filled Victoria sponge — then drizzle the warm melted chocolate across the top and pile on the decorations. By the time you serve the cake, the chocolate should be melting the berries so that they are iced but not frozen. Everything may be on the slide. Perfect.

140ml double cream
100g good-quality white
  or milk chocolate
350g frozen mixed berries
1 good-quality shop-bought
  sponge cake
a selection of interesting
  edibles for decorating

Over to the Easter bunny

Treats and gifts

The Easter Bank Holiday weekend is the first time we've all had a break since the back end of last year and so it's a perfect opportunity to sit in traffic on a motorway. And then, when we've done with the cars, it's time to sit round a table together and eat some good food.

In the stores we take it as our cue to switch seasons. We'll have done some freshening up along the way, but now we really get going. It's a big weekend for visitors and family gatherings, egg hunts and days out, and so in the run-up and over the long weekend, we decorate with daffs and hyacinths, freesias and tulips. And with chocolate: from our own boxed eggs to colourful chocolate cockerels, bags of little eggs, stacks of giant eggs, fairy cakes dotted with eggs, fancy biscuits and beautiful boxes of chocolates, it's fair to say we have it covered on the chocolate and egg front.

It's a great time of year, with that feeling that we're through the worst and we've got it all to come. And even if the rain is lashing down and the plan to go walking has to be abandoned in favour of grouting the tiles in the bathroom, with any luck somebody has thought to cook a delicious lunch. Or they've even turned up with some home-made treats. Come on, it has to happen sometimes.

Home-made treats for Easter

Obviously, there are eggs and all things chocolate to take along as a gift if you're out and about over Easter. Also, flowers. As we know, spring — in the sense that we can finally remove some layers and enjoy the sunshine — is sometimes lagging behind the calendar, and there's nothing like something freshly picked or growing to remind us and our homes that it shouldn't be long now. Daffodils, bunched and beribboned, pots of hyacinth or narcissus bulbs with their green shoots peeping through, have spring written all over them.

But what if you are in the mood for making something? A simple, sugary biscuit has been a traditional Easter gift across Britain for centuries, with many regional variations on a basic theme of flour, butter and eggs.

Here, over the page, is one version for you to try. This is a light and buttery biscuit, good as it is but possibly improved by a teaspoonful of home-made lemon curd on top (see over).

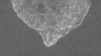

Shrewsbury biscuits

Preheat the oven to 180°C/160°C fan/gas mark 4 and prepare two baking sheets by lightly buttering them.

Cream the butter and sugar until pale, then add the egg yolks and beat well together. Add the finely grated lemon zest — or if you prefer an Easter spiced biscuit then use mixed spice instead of the lemon. Stir in the flour until you have a firm dough, then add the milk a little at a time, using your hands to make sure the mixture is sticking together well.

Roll the dough out on a floured board until it is ½ cm thick, cut out rounds with a 6cm cutter — or Easter bunny-shaped ones if you like — and arrange on the baking sheets.

Bake for about 15 minutes until the biscuits have turned a golden brown, and then transfer to a wire rack to cool.

* You could use the egg whites for the meringues on page 28 or the lemon meringue roulade on page 70.

125g unsalted butter,
 softened
150g caster sugar
2 egg yolks*
the zest of 1 lemon or
 1½ tsp mixed spice
225g plain flour, sifted
1-2 tbsp milk

Lemon curd

Even if you think you can't cook or make a thing — pastry, cakes, risotto — you'll be able to make lemon curd. So much quicker and less messy than making jam, it is easy-peasy-lemon-squeezy, and home-made has that real fresh lemon zing that you just don't get with shop-bought curd.

You can choose whether you use 4 whole eggs or 3 whole eggs and 1 egg yolk in this recipe — using a yolk in place of a whole egg gives a richer flavour and a deeper yellow curd.

MAKES 3 MEDIUM JARS

Use a bowl suspended over a pan of gently simmering water, or better still a double pan, if you have one. Melt the butter in the bowl, add all the other ingredients and stir with a wooden spoon to combine.

Keep the heat relatively low so the mixture doesn't boil and curdle. Keep gently stirring until the curd thickens and coats theback of the spoon. This shouldn't take long — maybe 15 minutes or so.

When it's ready, strain the lemon curd in to warm sterilized jars and seal. Kept in the fridge, it will last for 3 weeks, though it's so more-ish and such a lovely preserve to give away, it probably won't stay there that long.

110g unsalted butter, cubed
4 lemons, zested and juiced
4 eggs, lightly beaten
350g caster sugar

To sterilize jars, wash them in hot soapy water, rinse and shake off the excess water. Put them on a baking tray in a low oven for 10 minutes. Alternatively, you can run them through a hot wash in a dishwasher.

Slow-cooked lamb and beans

This is a great Bank Holiday weekend meal as it needs barely any attention once it's in the oven. It cooks quietly in the background for 4 hours while the kids are doing the Easter egg hunt and you sit with your feet up reading the paper. Oh no, sorry, that's what you wish you were doing. No, you are deciding whether or not you can get away with using the paint rollers you used last time, or maybe you should just get it over and done with and go to the DIY store, and at least then you can drop all that rubbish off at the dump on the way. Aah, the glamour that is a Bank Holiday.

Don't worry. A short blast of preparation and lunch is sorted for when you want to eat. Even better, with the addition of more beans or some potatoes tucked in to bake alongside the roast, it will stretch to feed a party, should one happen to turn up.

SERVES 6

Preheat the oven to 150°C/130°C fan/gas mark 2.

Season the lamb with salt and freshly ground black pepper, then slice half the garlic cloves in quarters, make incisions in the lamb and stuff the garlic quarters in. Heat the olive oil in a large roasting tin, put the garlic-studded lamb in the oven and get it good and brown on all sides, probably about 5 minutes per side. Remove the lamb and set aside.

Place the remaining garlic cloves, the chopped vegetables and the rosemary and thyme in the roasting tin and brown them over a medium heat for about 5 minutes, stirring occasionally.

Add the tomatoes, wine and stock to the roasting tin and bring to a simmer. Put the lamb on top, skin side down. Cover the dish with foil and place it in the oven for 2 hours.

After 2 hours, take the roasting tin out of the oven and remove the lamb. Stir the beans in to the tomato-vegetable-stock mixture, put the lamb back on top, skin side up this time, and replace the foil. Return the roasting tin to the oven for a further hour. After 45 minutes, remove the foil, add the halved garlic bulbs (if using) and cook everything for another 30 minutes.

Take the roasting tin out of the oven, remove the lamb and leave it on a board to rest, loosely covered with foil, for 20-30 minutes. Meanwhile, remove the excess fat from the roasting tin – tipping it gently will allow the film of fat to pool in the lowest corner, making it easier to spoon off. Season the beans and vegetables and stir in a handful of chopped parsley and most of the lemon zest. Serve topped with the lamb and garnished with a few sprigs of fresh rosemary, the remaining lemon zest and parsley and with the roasted garlic halves if you've included them.

1 shoulder or leg of lamb, bone in (approx. 2.2kg)
1 bulb of garlic, cloves separated and peeled
2 tbsp olive oil
2 large carrots, peeled and sliced
2 sticks of celery, sliced
1 leek, peeled and sliced
2 medium onions, diced
2 large parsnips, peeled, cut in half and sliced
3 sprigs of fresh rosemary, plus extra to garnish
3 sprigs of fresh thyme
1 x 400g tin of chopped plum tomatoes
300ml red wine
300ml lamb or chicken stock
2 x 400g tins of cannelloni or flageolet beans, rinsed and drained
2 bulbs of garlic, halved, to roast for garnish (optional)
1 small bunch of flat-leaf parsley, roughly chopped
the zest of 1 lemon

Lemon meringue roulade

Looks tricky, really isn't and so this is the pudding for Easter Sunday. If you want to, you can make it a couple of days ahead and keep it wrapped in the fridge, ready to present at the right moment.

Preheat the oven to 200°C/180°C fan/gas mark 6 and line a 23 x 33cm Swiss roll tin with a sheet of baking parchment.

Whisk the egg whites till stiff and glossy, then gradually add the sugar a spoonful at a time, whisking between each spoonful until all the sugar has been added.

Spread the mixture evenly over the baking parchment, smooth it with a spatula and gently tap it down a few times on the worktop to get it even. Sprinkle with the flaked almonds.

Bake for 10 minutes or until the meringue just starts to turn a golden colour, turn the oven down to 160°C/140°C fan/gas mark 3 and continue baking for a further 20 minutes.

Remove from the oven and rest the meringue for 5 minutes before carefully turning the almond side down on to another piece of baking parchment. Leave to cool for a further 10-15 minutes.

Meanwhile, gently fold the lemon curd and crème fraîche together so you get a lovely marbled effect and when the meringue is cool, spread this mixture over it.

Next, roll up the meringue tightly and firmly, using the paper to help you. It is important to be brave at this point and not to worry if the roulade starts to crack a little – this just adds to the divine nature of this heavenly pudding.

Chill well before you serve with a generous dusting of icing sugar and some fresh berries. The berry coulis on page 110 goes very well here, drizzled over each serving.

* For what to do with the egg yolks, see page 26 for hollandaise sauce and page 66 for Shrewsbury biscuits and lemon curd.

4 egg whites*
250g caster sugar
50g flaked almonds
6 tbsp lemon curd
300ml crème fraîche
icing sugar, to dust
fresh berries, to serve

So, we're done with Easter, then.
The children have gone back to school
and there are days when you step outside
and can just tell — from the birds, from
the heat of the sun and the light, from the
new colours and a scent of something in
the air, that we're off to pastures new and
it won't be long until we tip, happily, in
to summer.

'We've packed for all eventualities.' I love that. It says everything about the British attitude to summer, because it's all and only ever about the weather. What it means is, whether there are floods, howling gales or blistering sunshine, we've got it covered. From windbreaks to wellies and sunshades, it's all somehow been stuffed in to the car. And we all have a good laugh and feel a bit pleased with ourselves, as if nobody's ever been quite that ingenious.

In spite of the complete unpredictability of the British summer, we throw ourselves at it with optimism – planning weddings and garden parties, holidays and picnics on the beach. Quite right too, because when the sun does shine, on those days that begin with a mist and a promising warmth in the air and end with lingering over supper in the garden way after the sun has set, it makes up for all the times we've sat huddled in steamy cafés or held a pair of barbecue tongs in one hand and an umbrella in the other.

And, reassuringly, even when the weather does let us down, summer's fresh produce always delivers. From bright and fresh salad leaves and herbs to berries, currants and stone fruits, beans and tomatoes, we're rolling in variety and abundance from June right through the summer and well in to late autumn.

This is the season for throwing quick and easy dishes together – fresh salads that mix up the flavours and textures, puddings that revolve around fruit and something creamy, good sandwiches and clinking jugs of juices and cordials. The emphasis should be on fast and flavoursome food that can be just as easily packed in to bags as piled on to trays for eating in the garden.

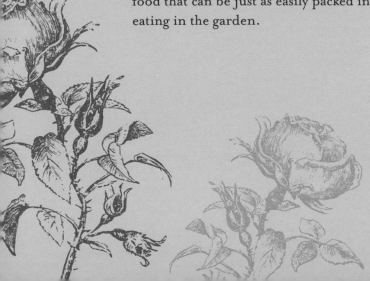

Bill's

SUMMER CHAMPIONS

There's plenty to sing about during the summer and here are our seasonal favourites — delicious, colourful and overflowing on a plate near you.

And out in to the sunshine we go

Tomatoes
Fruits of the vine

It's not so long ago that tomatoes went through an extended period in the doldrums and markets were full of tasteless, insipid-looking, uniformly shaped specimens. But, happily, those dark days are behind us and the tomato is back to its fruity, colourful, flavourful self. There's still a bit too much uniformity, but we can't have it all, and as they're so easy to grow, we can create the weird and wonderful in our back gardens and on windowsills, if we like.

A home-grown superfood, tomatoes pack a health-giving punch and make a brilliant jumping-off point for so many dishes. In the cafés, we roast them in the oven to intensify the flavour and then use them in soup, pasta, meat and fish dishes and risotto, as well as in salads and sandwiches.

When there's a glut — and if you're growing tomatoes at home, there's almost always a glut — you need never get tired of them, because they're so amenable. Chutney, sauces for pasta, soup and sticky chickeny casseroles all love tomatoes. In fact there's good reason to eat them at every mealtime, which you could easily do if you're partial to fried or grilled tomatoes on toast with a sprinkle of salt for breakfast.

For lunch, whizz them in to a soup (see recipe on page 86) or throw them in to a salad with avocado and rocket and a good mustardy dressing. Then, for supper, the following dishes will help to complete a tomato-fuelled day.

Some quick and easy tomato ideas

 Tray-baked tomatoes

Chop tomatoes – all sorts and sizes – and put in an ovenproof tray, then stir them together with unpeeled whole garlic cloves (as few or as many as you like), fresh herbs such as rosemary, oregano or thyme, some sea salt and a good slug of olive oil. Place the tray in the oven at about 160°C/140°C fan/gas mark 3 and bake slowly to reduce the tomatoes down to a really rich goo – this will take anything up to an hour. You can shake the tray around now and then during the cooking or just keep an eye out to make sure nothing burns. These roasted tomatoes are very good with any fish, fowl or meat. You can also spread them over the pastry base of a quiche before adding the filling, or layer them up on some good bread that's been toasted (squeezing the garlic purée out of the skins first).

Tomatoes and pasta

Baby tomatoes are great in pasta. Wilt them in a pan with some olive oil or grill them till they're just softening, or tray-bake them (see page 83) then tip them in to cooked pasta. You can keep things really simple and just finish them off with Parmesan, salt and black pepper or you can add other flourishes, such as some anchovies, olives or torn basil leaves, but those little toms, bursting sweetly and juicily in your mouth, argue the less-is-more theory pretty soundly.

Good workaday lunch

This lily needs no gilding. The old cheese and tomato combination has been filling faces for hundreds of years, not just here but anywhere that has the sunshine and rain needed for a healthy tomato vine. My choice would be a big hunk of fresh sourdough, a ball of mozzarella or some strong Cheddar, a bottle of good olive oil, a brown paper bag of ripe tomatoes and a box of Maldon sea salt.

Tomatoes love…

lots of other flavours and textures, but especially olive oil, balsamic, olives, pasta, chicken, bacon, anchovies, eggs, garlic and onions.

Waste not, want not

Place green tomatoes in a thick paper bag or cardboard box with a ripening fruit, such as an apple or a banana. Check every day and remove the tomatoes that have ripened – and replace the apple or banana if needs be. They might take a few weeks, but all the tomatoes should eventually turn red. Otherwise, it's the chutney pot for them (see recipe on opposite page).

To sterilize jars, wash them in hot soapy water, rinse and shake off the excess water. Put them on a baking tray in a low oven for 10 minutes. Alternatively, you can run them through a hot wash in a dishwasher.

To skin tomatoes, score a little cross in the base of each tomato and put them in to a heatproof bowl. Pour boiling water over the tomatoes, enough to cover them. Leave them in the hot water just long enough for the skin to wrinkle and split – about 15-20 seconds. Lift the tomatoes out of the hot water with a slotted spoon and transfer them to a bowl of cold water. Let them sit till they're cool enough to handle, when you should find the skin will easily peel away.

Really quite saucy fresh tomato sauce

Ripe plum vine tomatoes are best for flavour and texture. Cook up a batch of this robust sauce for pasta, pizza, soups and all sorts. Use some of it straight away, keep some of it in the fridge to use over the next few days, and bottle or freeze the rest for a taste of summer goodness when sunny days are just a memory.

MAKES 4 JARS

Heat the oil in a large pan, cook the onion and celery gently until they're just turning translucent — about 7 or 8 minutes or so — and then add the slivered garlic and cook for another couple of minutes. Add all the remaining ingredients apart from the tomato purée and basil leaves, and simmer for about 7-10 minutes until the tomatoes are soft and the sauce has reduced and thickened. You may not need any purée, depending on the richness of the flavour of the tomatoes — taste the sauce and add it if necessary, together with salt and freshly ground black pepper. Take out and discard the chilli, tear the basil leaves and stir them in to finish.

2 tbsp olive oil
3 small onions, finely diced
I stick of celery, finely diced
3 garlic cloves, sliced as thinly
  as possible
Ikg tomatoes, skinned and chopped
I red chilli, split but kept whole
275ml white wine
2 tsp honey
2 bay leaves
½ tsp fennel seeds
2 tsp dried oregano
2 tbsp tomato purée (optional)
a handful of basil leaves

Betty Webb's hot tomato chutney

Betty Webb was my wife Becca's granny. Becca says to emphasize that this chutney is HOT and to vary the number of chillies you use according to taste.

MAKES 4-5 JARS

Place the tomatoes in a large colander with some sea salt and leave them to sit for 30 minutes to let some of the juice drain out. Then tip them in to a large, heavy-based pan.

Add all the other ingredients, then cook everything together slowly for 1½-2 hours, stirring every so often to make sure it doesn't burn, until the chutney is dark and thick. Check and adjust the seasoning if you think it needs it.

Leave to stand for 10-15 minutes, then pour in to sterilized, warm jars. Seal and leave to set.

It's best to store chutney for a minimum of 3 months before eating, to allow the flavours to mature (if you eat it too early, it may taste a bit vinegary).

2½kg tomatoes, quartered
150ml cider vinegar
225g onions, sliced
225g Bramley apples, peeled,
  cored and cut in to chunks
700g demerara sugar
½ tsp cayenne pepper
½ tsp ground cloves
7 dried Kashmiri and
  3 fresh chillies, deseeded
  and roughly chopped

Roast tomato and orange soup

A great summer soup that can be eaten hot or cold, gazpacho-style. It's very good for using up lots of tomatoes, either your own or ones you've bought cheaply at the height of their season.

SERVES 4

Preheat the oven to 180°C/160°C fan/gas mark 4.

Put the tomatoes on a large baking tray and scatter with the chopped garlic. Drizzle with 2 tablespoons of olive oil and season with salt and a grind or two of black pepper. Place the tomatoes in the oven and roast for 45 minutes, stirring once halfway through.

After you've stirred the tomatoes, heat the remaining olive oil in a large, deep-sided pan and cook the onions, carrots and celery over a low heat for 20 minutes. Tip in the roasted tomatoes and garlic, add the stock and orange juice to the pan and give everything a good stir.

Bring the soup to a simmer for a minute or two, then take it off the heat and allow it to cool slightly before liquidizing. Return the soup to the pan and check the seasoning, adding more salt and freshly ground black pepper to taste. If you're serving it immediately, make sure it's properly heated through.

If you're going to serve the soup cold, let it cool completely, pour in to a large container and chill for a couple of hours in the fridge.

Serve with a pinch of orange zest and, if you feel like it, decorate with some fresh edible flowers such as borage or nasturtium.

900g tomatoes, halved
  (small ones left whole)
2 garlic cloves, finely chopped
4 tbsp olive oil
2 onions, diced
2 carrots, peeled or scrubbed
  and diced
1 stick of celery, diced
560ml hot vegetable stock
100ml orange juice
the zest of 1 small orange,
  to serve
edible flowers, to serve
  (optional)

Beans

Bean there, done that

Runners, French, flat, green, bobby, broad, purple — whichever, they're all plentiful throughout the summer. Whether you're growing them in the garden or on your allotment or getting good bean bargains in shops and markets, you should make the most of them right through the season.

Use them raw or blanched (briskly boiled until just cooked through, a minute or two depending on how finely you've sliced them, and then plunged in to iced water so they keep their flavour, crunch and colour). Add them, sliced or shredded, to salads. They're very good in pasta salads with a handful of sun-dried tomatoes and crumbled feta cheese.

For dressings, they're good with anything involving mustard and lemon juice, crème fraîche, olive oil and plenty of freshly ground black pepper. Cooked, they especially like onions, garlic, tomatoes and chilli, as well as other summery vegetables and herbs.

If you're growing beans and they're all peaking at once, you'll need some ideas up your sleeve. Simplest is to stir-fry sliced beans with some garlic and two or three chopped fresh tomatoes. Finish off with a drizzle of olive oil, a sprinkle of salt and a squeeze of lemon. This works as a side dish or you can turn it in to the main event with some rice or a baked potato and plenty of grated cheese.

 ## Bean feast

Start by finely chopping an onion or two, which you cook gently
in a pan with a dash of olive oil as you prepare the beans. Use
as many different types as you like – so pod broad beans, slice
runners, top and tail French beans etc.

The more you have to use up, the bigger the pan, as this dish
will run and run. Add some finely chopped garlic to the onions,
let them fry together for a couple of minutes and then tip in the
beans. Keep stirring as you go, adding a good sprinkle of sea
salt, until things are cooked to how you like them – from crunchy
right through to almost melted down (which I prefer).

Remove the pan from the heat and allow everything to cool a little.
Stir in a generous slug of good olive oil and crumble some feta over
the top. Serve warm alongside roast chicken or grilled fish. You
can also eat this cold as a salad and the dish will keep happily in
the fridge for several days.

Beetroot

Sweet, purple fruits of the earth

As a strong flavour, beetroot needs to be matched, which is why the tart acidity of orange juice works (see the winter juice boost on page 269). Strong, salty cheeses also go well with beetroot — feta, halloumi and blue cheeses especially. Try the recipe on page 140 for a goat's cheese and roast beetroot salad. Salads involving roast beetroot are all the rage and for good reason. Beetroot are easy to roast as you just put them on a baking tray, skins on, and in to a fairly hot oven (200°C/180°C fan/gas mark 6) for 45 minutes. You can wrap them loosely in foil or drizzle with oil if you like, but really they're fine as they are. Test to see if they're cooked through by running a knife in to them. When they're done, allow them to cool for a while and then peel off the skins, which should slip off really easily. Cube, slice or grate the beetroot in to a salad — lovely with oranges and watercress.

Young beetroot leaves can also be shredded in to salads, while the older ones can be steamed or stir-fried like chard. In fact the two belong to the same family — it's just that chard is grown for the leaves and beetroot for the bulb.

Finally, if you'd really like to turn heads on the beetroot front, look out for some of the more fancy ones. Some are revivals of old English varieties, others are from continental Europe, such as the Chioggia, which looks just like an ordinary beetroot until you slice in to it to reveal the alternate red and white rings. This looks lovely sliced thinly in to a salad, as does the golden beetroot, which is a bright sunshine yellow and has a milder, sweeter taste.

Beetroot pesto

It's unlikely you will want to turn the oven on just to roast a single beetroot, but if you happen to be roasting some for a salad you could add an extra one so you can try this delicious, vibrantly coloured pesto. Use it as you would a basil pesto — to dress pasta, for bruschetta or spread on toast, topped with cheese and grilled. You can also spread it on the pastry base of quiches before you add the filling.

MAKES ONE SMALL BOWLFUL

Roughly chop the beetroot and put in a blender along with all the other ingredients. Blend for just long enough to create a textured pesto — if you want it more liquid, simply blend with additional olive oil until you reach the desired consistency. Season to taste with salt and freshly ground black pepper.

This will keep for a few days in the fridge in a sealed jam jar.

1 medium beetroot, roasted, cooled and peeled
1 garlic clove, crushed
30g pine nuts, toasted
30g Parmesan, grated
1 tsp sesame oil
2 tsp olive oil (or more, to taste)
a handful of basil leaves, torn

Beetroot, cheese and potato pie

A savoury big hitter and a Bill's classic, this is a very good recipe for using up bits and bobs of cheese, as you really can add whatever you have in the fridge. Cheddar is the obvious choice, but you can use Stilton or other strong blue cheeses too. Throw at it what you will, the beetroot can handle it. Using ready-made pastry will speed up the process too.

SERVES 8 AS A STARTER, 4 AS A MAIN COURSE

Preheat the oven to 180°C/160°C fan/gas mark 4 and leave a baking sheet in the oven to get hot. You will need a muffin tin with 12 holes or a 20-23cm flan tin.

Roll out the pastry to line the flan tin or cut in to 12 circles to line the muffin cups, pressing gently in to the base. Prick the base of the flan tin or muffin cups with a fork, place a piece of baking parchment in to each round of pastry and fill with baking beans or rice. Place on to the hot baking sheet in the oven and bake for 10 minutes (15 minutes for the large pie). Remove the beans and baking parchment, then return the tin to the oven for a further 5 minutes, until the pastry turns golden brown. Remove and set aside.

In a large pan, add the olive oil and cook the onion over a low heat for 5 minutes, then add the garlic and cook for a further minute. Add the potatoes, milk and cream and slowly bring to a simmer. Continue to simmer gently for 15-20 minutes, till the potatoes are cooked through. Keep an eye on the pan to make sure the mixture doesn't catch and burn.

Remove the pan from the heat and add three-quarters of the grated cheese, the grated beetroot, roughly three-quarters of the chives and a twist or two of black pepper. Fold everything together — it will be bright pink — and check the seasoning. Spoon the mixture in to the pastry cases and sprinkle with the rest of the grated cheese and the crumbled feta. Return the pies to the oven for 10 minutes until the cheese is melted and bubbling on top (15 minutes for the larger pie).

Scatter with the remaining chopped chives and serve with a green salad.

375g shortcrust pastry
1 tbsp olive oil
1 medium onion, diced
1 garlic clove, finely chopped
200g waxy potatoes, peeled and thinly sliced
140ml milk
140ml double cream
175g cheese, grated
2 large raw beetroot (approx. 250g), peeled and coarsely grated
a handful of chives, roughly chopped
100g feta cheese, crumbled

Beetroot and chocolate cake

One of beetroot's most unexpected companions is chocolate. If you haven't tried a chocolate and beetroot cake before, now's the time. Not just for the amazing colour — rich chocolate shot through with purple — but also because the two flavours go so well together. Perhaps surprisingly, given that beetroot has a strong flavour, it doesn't overwhelm at all. Instead, it brings a rich and moist earthiness to proceedings and makes for many a double-take as people try to guess the secret ingredient.

Boil the beetroot in water until it's tender to the point of a knife, probably about 30 minutes. Drain and allow it to cool for 30 minutes or so, then remove the skin and coarsely grate the beetroot.

Preheat the oven to 180°C/160°C fan/gas mark 4, and prepare two cake tins (20cm in diameter) by lightly buttering them and lining with baking parchment.

Beat the sugar, eggs and oil together, either by hand or in a food processor. Add the grated beetroot and cocoa and blend well. Finally, sift in the flour and bicarbonate of soda and mix again. Divide the mixture between the cake tins, smoothing down flat.

Bake for about 35 minutes, until the cakes feel springy to the touch. Remove from the oven, let them stand for 15 minutes and then gently turn out on to a wire rack.

While the cakes cool, make the butter-cream filling. Sift the icing sugar and cocoa together, beat in the butter, drizzle in the milk and beat some more. Add a little more milk if you think it's needed: you want the filling to be very smooth and to hold its shape.

When the cakes are completely cold, lay each one flat side up. Spread one with the butter cream and the other with cherry jam, then sandwich the two together. It's always a bonus when the cream and jam ooze out of the sides a little. Finally, generously dust the top with icing sugar.

FOR THE CAKE

3 medium beetroot
  (approx. 300g)
300g caster sugar
3 large eggs
250ml vegetable oil
75g cocoa powder
250g self-raising flour
1½ tsp bicarbonate of soda

FOR THE FILLING

200g icing sugar, plus
  extra for dusting
1 tbsp cocoa powder
100g unsalted butter, softened
2 tbsp cold milk
2 generous tbsp cherry jam

Garlic
Flash bulb

When I was a kid, we didn't have garlic. Hard to believe, isn't it? We didn't have olive oil, avocados, couscous, chorizo, rocket or balsamic vinegar either. I could go on… I mean, we barely had pasta or Parmesan. They're all ingredients I love and, OK, I can imagine life without them, but it would be weird in the kitchen. Especially having no garlic.

For a start, garlic has to be one of the best, most welcoming smells: think of a garlicky chicken roasting in the oven. And for something so distinctive, the taste covers quite a spectrum, from the almost eye-watering punch of fresh garlic rubbed across toast, right through to the sweet, unctuous warmth of cloves roasted in their skins till they're as soft as a purée.

Pan con tomate

The classic Spanish breakfast dish. Eaten in a noisy corner café in Granada or halfway up a mountainside with the sound of goat bells and the scent of thyme would be perfect, but a glimpse of summer through a kitchen window is a good second best.

Toast some bread – the more rustic the better. Peel and halve a garlic clove and lightly rub the cut half across the toasted bread. Slice a ripe tomato in two and rub half across the toast. It doesn't matter if it's all a bit messy. The idea is to let the toast absorb the flavour and juices. Finish with a drizzle of good olive oil, a sprinkle of salt and a grinding of black pepper.

Roast garlic

Add garlic cloves, skins on, to just about any meat or vegetables that are roasting in the oven for some time – say, at least 30 minutes. Cooked for long enough, the cloves turn in to little pods of garlic purée that you can spread on to bread, add to gravies and creamy sauces or, mostly – if it's me cooking – squeeze straight in to the mouth. Oh, come on, garlic's good for you!

Wet garlic

New season's garlic, known as wet garlic, is sweet and delicate in flavour, which means it can be used raw more liberally than the stronger-tasting older garlic. Thinly slice it in salads, especially with tomatoes and herbs, or crush it in to a lemony dressing.

Pickled garlic

Look out for pickled garlic in Bill's stores or at your local deli. Great with any mezze dish, added to marinating olives, stirred through pasta or mixed in with salads, pickled garlic delivers crunch and a softened garlicky hit. Keep a supply in the fridge and add to any number of hot and cold dishes.

Mint

Mint summer madness

Because we use mint all year round in the cafés, I can and do drink fresh mint tea pretty much all the time — a few torn leaves in a cup, topped up with hot water, steeped for a bit and you're away. It's soothing and refreshing all at the same time — like a shower on the inside.

But tea is just the beginning of what you can do with this aromatic herb, as mint adds a fresh and fragrant energy to many dishes, sweet and savoury. In the UK, it's the obvious accompaniment to new potatoes and lamb, sometimes added to summery drinks or to a fruit salad, but across Africa, the Middle East and Asia, mint is added to all sorts, from salads and curries to tagines and desserts.

If you're growing it in the garden, you will already know mint can grow like a weed once it's taken hold. You may well be wanting to find as many minty miracles as you can get your hands on, to make the most of it while it's in season.

 Mint and yoghurt

Stir mint through yoghurt and add peeled, finely diced cucumber for simple tzatziki and raita, which create a cooling foil for fiery or rich dishes. From a base of these two ingredients, you can also play with other fruits and flavours to make dishes that work equally well as side dishes for savoury meals or as light and refreshing puddings. Try adding melon, orange segments or pomegranate seeds, or toasted nuts, rosewater, cinnamon and honey – though maybe not all together.

Mint and chocolate

All those after-dinner mints can't be wrong: there's something about mint and chocolate – it's another horse and carriage job.

In the café we serve hot chocolate using a Spanish chocolate powder, El Canario, which has cinnamon and vanilla in it as well as toasted cocoa, but you can use any brand. To add the hint of mint, infuse some hot milk with a stem or two of fresh mint leaves for 5 minutes, then discard the mint and reheat the milk, whisking in the hot chocolate powder according to the instructions on the tin. A swirl of cream on the top and a sprig of mint will complete the moment.

Berries

Bring on the berries

Years ago, I used to go to the markets and there would be growers there with a few boxes of strawberries, along with other boxes of this and that, whatever was in season, and you bartered. Some days you got a better deal than others, but so did they, and it all worked in the way things did in the days when keeping up with technology meant having a pencil behind your ear.

You could also buy berries from makeshift stalls set up by the side of the road and pick your own on many more farms than you can today. Oh, the old pick-your-own experience — eat one, one for the basket, eat one, one for the basket… until you felt the sort of queasy you get from eating a summer's worth of strawberries in two hours. Then it was home in the car with hands stained red and the sweet, jammy scent of berries hanging heavily. Happy days.

Then English strawberries just about disappeared, squeezed out by the supermarkets pushing for cheaper prices, and the market was flooded by Dutch and Belgian berries, all looking like they were made on the lathe — no more roadside stalls, no more pick-your-own.

But, as with so many things, it's all a-changing and the English strawberry is making a comeback. So, in our duty to support our local growers, we should all eat as many as we can during the season.

A summer's bowl o' granola with fresh berries

Taking time to smell the roses — literally and metaphorically — is a very good way to start the day. And summer's warmer mornings mean we can open the door and wander outside to find a spot to eat breakfast. The sun has been up for a lot longer than most of us, heating that bench or wall, so take advantage by sitting outside and eating something delicious — even if it's just for 5 minutes.

What to have for an outdoor breakfast? Well, I'm thinking fresh summer berries along with something quick and healthy, sustaining and flavoursome that you can spoon out of a jar without having to think too much. Yes, it has to be granola.

The good thing about granola — one of the good things — is that you can make each batch according to what you feel like. Love dried apricots? Add plenty. Looking for something a bit luxurious? Throw in a bag of chocolate chips or macadamia nuts. The important part is to hone the basic recipe and then, each time you make it, play around with the extras.

Eat it with yoghurt or milk or even juice if you prefer. Add fruit — fresh or stewed, a drizzle of honey or maple syrup, whatever takes your fancy, and then head off, bowl in hand, barefoot in to the garden.

Good garden granola

MAKES ROUGHLY 500G

Preheat the oven to 120°C/100°C fan/gas mark ½.

Gently warm the honey, vanilla extract, oil, butter and sugar together in a small pan. When the honey is nicely runny and the sugar has melted, take the pan off the heat and add 2 tablespoons of cold water.

Put all the dry ingredients in a bowl and add the honey mixture. Stir thoroughly to make sure that everything is well coated, then spread over a large shallow baking tray lined with baking parchment. Bake for 50 minutes, stirring every 15 minutes or so to ensure the granola browns evenly and to stop it sticking to the tray.

Remove the tray from the oven and allow the granola to cool completely. This is the moment to add chopped dried apricots, dried blueberries or cranberries, if you like, before storing in an airtight jar.

2 tbsp honey
1 tbsp vanilla extract
1 tbsp sunflower oil
1 generous knob of butter
40g light brown sugar
220g jumbo oats
150g chopped mixed nuts (any or all of brazils, almonds, peanuts)
60g mixed seeds (pumpkin, sunflower, linseed)

Berry brioches

Good any time of day, this combination of textures and flavours gives a different take on cream tea, is a quick and delicious pudding and makes a lovely breakfast for a summer morning. Allow two slices of brioche for each person.

SERVES 4

In a large bowl mix together the berries and sugar. Mash lightly with a fork and leave for 5 minutes.

In another bowl mix together the yoghurt, mascarpone, lemon zest and juice and set aside.

Cut the brioche in to thick-ish slices and toast on both sides.

To serve, put a heaped tablespoon of mixed berries, a dollop of the mascarpone mix and a drizzle of honey on top of each slice of brioche.

200g mixed berries
25g caster sugar
125g Greek yoghurt
125g mascarpone cheese
the zest and juice of 1 lemon
1 brioche loaf
  (approx. 400g)
2 tbsp honey

Raspberry Eve's pudding

Whereas strawberries can be a bit tarty — and yes, I do mean it like that — raspberries, more subtle in colour and flavour, are their demure cousins, sitting in the shade and being a bit sophisticated. They're delicious fresh, of course, but cooking intensifies the flavour and when you add a light sponge and some cream, I think it's fair to say we're talking very sexy food indeed.

SERVES 4–6

Preheat the oven to 180°C/160°C fan/gas mark 4.

Sift the flour and baking powder in to a large bowl or food processor. Add the butter, sugar and eggs and blitz until the mixture is glossy. Add 2 tablespoons of water, a bit at a time, if you think you need it, to make a soft dropping consistency.

Place the berries in an ovenproof dish, add a splash of water and a generous tablespoon of caster sugar. Spoon the sponge mixture over the berries and smooth the top.

Place the dish in the oven and bake for 20–25 minutes, until the top is golden and springy. Remove from the oven, sprinkle with the remaining caster sugar and let the pudding sit for a good 10 minutes. A jug of cream nearby will make the dish — and you — sing.

125g self-raising flour
1 tsp baking powder
125g butter, softened
125g caster sugar,
   plus 2 tbsp
2 medium eggs
500g raspberries

Time to celebrate!

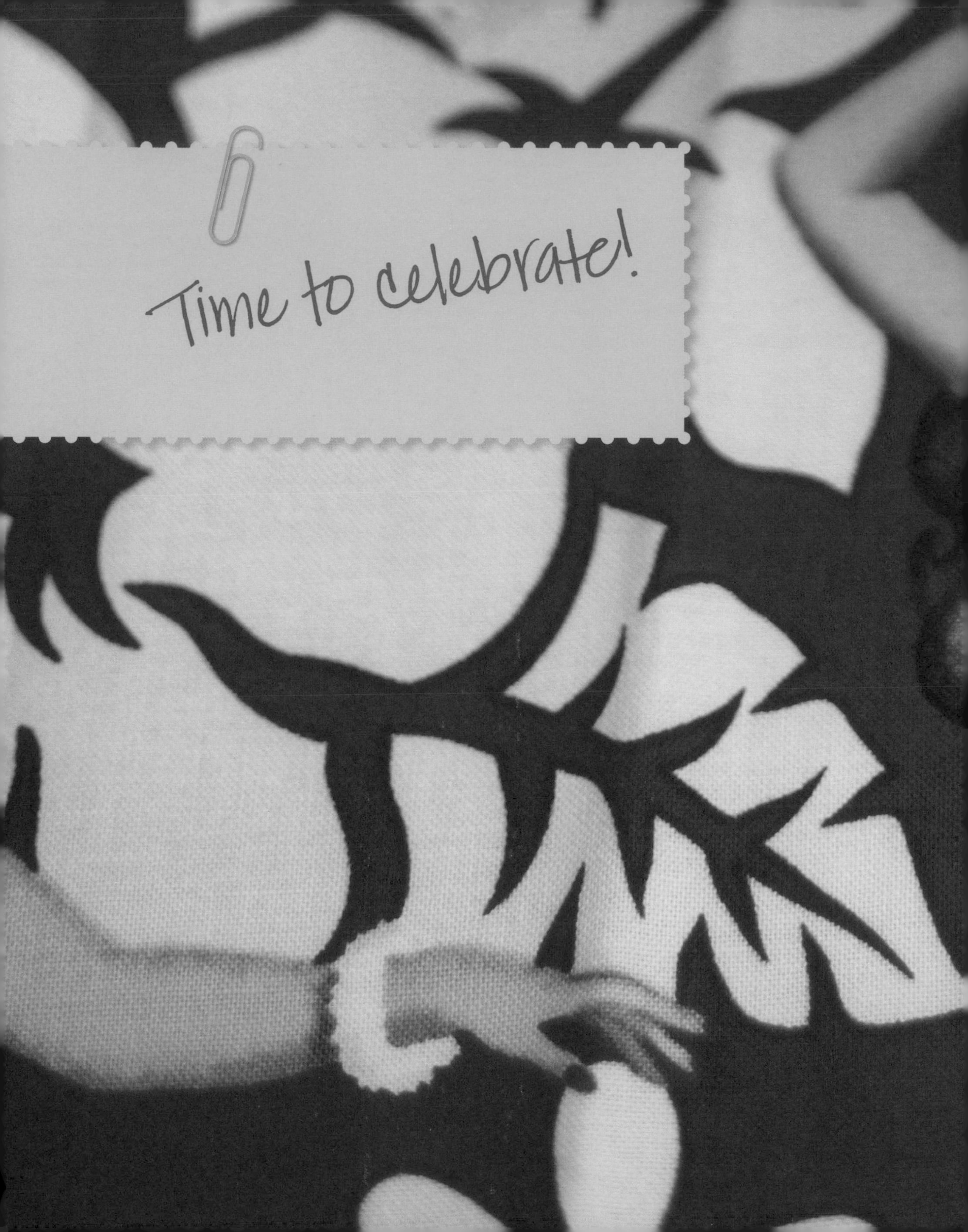

Summer pavlova with a berry coulis

There are times, like birthdays and anniversaries, welcoming loved ones and seeing them off again, passing exams and getting new jobs, when we just have to celebrate and what's called for is a sense of occasion.

So, hang out the bunting and balloons, fill some fluted glasses with something fizzy and make either this dessert or the cake on the following page.

SERVES 8

Preheat the oven to 140°C/120°C fan/gas mark 1.

In a large clean bowl, whisk the egg whites until they form soft peaks and then gradually add the sugar, whisking as you go until you have glossy, marshmallow-like peaks. Fold in the cornflour, vinegar and vanilla extract.

Cover a large baking tray with baking parchment and spoon the meringue on to the paper, creating pretty much whatever shape you like, building up the sides to create a shallow bowl. Slide in to the oven and bake for 1½ hours, then turn off the heat and leave the meringue until the oven is completely cool. Ideally, if you can, this should be overnight.

When you are ready to assemble the pavlova, peel the baking parchment away from the bottom of the meringue and place it on a serving plate.

Break the chocolate in to pieces and put in a bowl over a pan of simmering water. When the chocolate has melted, use it to coat the inside of the meringue and then put in a cool place until the chocolate has set.

Take the fruit and berries for the topping. Cut the fruit in chunks and tidy the berries up, cutting some of the larger strawberries in half and leaving some whole. Whip the cream in a large bowl until it forms soft peaks, gently fold in the vanilla extract and pile the whipped cream in to the chocolate-coated meringue base. Arrange the fruit and berries in a non-arranged sort of way all over the cream.

For the coulis, put the berries in a pan with the caster sugar. Bring slowly to the boil, then simmer very gently for 5 minutes. Allow to cool slightly before sieving in to a jug, ready for pouring.

When you are ready to serve the pavlova, decorate the top however you fancy it, with chocolate sticks or mint leaves and flowers – geraniums or marigolds look particularly pretty – and dust generously with icing sugar.

FOR THE MERINGUE BASE
3 large egg whites
175g caster sugar
2 tsp cornflour
1 level tsp white wine
  vinegar
1 tsp vanilla extract

FOR THE TOPPING
200g white chocolate
500g mixed fruit
  and berries
400ml double cream
2 tsp vanilla extract

FOR THE COULIS
250g mixed berries
1 tbsp caster sugar

TO DECORATE
chocolate sticks (optional)
fresh mint and flowers
  (optional)
icing sugar, to dust

If there are roses to be cut — from your garden, from the hedgerow — this is the cake to make for summer birthdays. Or, indeed, any time that requires a cake resplendent in cream, berries and pink icing. The cake itself is pretty straightforward and the devil — as with most of what we do at Bill's — is in the detail and the finishing flourishes.

The quantities here are suitable for two Victoria sponges. If you would like to make a three-tiered cake, as in our picture, you will need to add half as much again of all the ingredients.

Preheat the oven to 180°C/160°C fan/gas mark 4, then lightly butter two cake tins 20cm in diameter and line with baking parchment.

In a large mixing bowl, beat the sugar and butter together till they are pale and fluffy. Gradually add the beaten egg a little at a time. If the mixture starts to curdle, add a teaspoon of flour and this should bring it back together. Add the vanilla extract.

Mix in the baking powder and half the flour, then fold in the rest. Divide the mixture between the cake tins. Smooth the tops, then bake for 20-25 minutes. The cakes should be nicely risen and the sponge should spring back when you press a finger on to it and should have shrunk away slighty from the sides of the tin. Leave the cakes in their tins for 10 minutes before turning out on to a wire cooling rack.

Meanwhile, whisk the double cream until it stands in soft peaks, adding the rosewater as you go. Then fold in the raspberry jam, being careful not to over-mix, as you want to create a ripple effect.

When the cakes are completely cool, turn one of them flat base uppermost, slather with the cream mixture and scatter with raspberries, slightly crushed. Top with the second cake. If you've made three cakes, spread more cream and raspberries over the second layer and top with the third.

For the pink glacé icing, mix together the icing sugar, water and rosewater, and stir in the juice from a few crushed raspberries until it's all looking gloriously pink. Drizzle the rose icing across the cake and don't worry if things are looking a little tipsy. Allow jam, cream, berries and icing to slide if they want to — within reason.

Arrange the roses, dot with rose petals and the remaining raspberries and dust with icing sugar. If you have any edible silver dust, now's the time. Scatter with silver stars too if you have them, but just a few.

Finally, cake stand, flutes of kir royale or pink lemonade and/or very delicate cups of tea to serve. Cue out of tune, out of step, somewhat uncomfortable — in a very English sort of way — rendition of 'Happy Birthday'.

FOR THE CAKE

- 225g golden caster sugar
- 225g unsalted butter, softened
- 4 medium eggs, beaten
- 1 tsp vanilla extract
- 1 tsp baking powder
- 225g self-raising flour, sifted

FOR THE ROSE-CREAM FILLING

- 300ml double cream
- rosewater
- raspberry jam
- 250g fresh raspberries

FOR THE ROSE GLACÉ ICING

- icing sugar
- water
- rosewater

TO DECORATE

- roses
- fresh raspberries
- icing sugar

Currants

Anyone for tennis?

Along with gooseberries, blackcurrants are an old-fashioned, English country garden sort of fruit and it's a shame they make such a brief appearance these days. You'll find a few punnets at the height of the summer, but the bulk of the British crop is bottled for squash.

But, the bushes are tidy and you could fit a few in to a corner of a garden or a tub on a veranda for your own little crop, covering them with some netting so the birds don't get to them first. And when it does come to picking them, this really ought to be done only by women called Audrey and Lydia wearing battered sunhats just before luncheon on a Sunday and it should be the 1930s and all the family are there and getting on jolly nicely and some of them are playing tennis.

And then the currants are turned in to a purple-juiced pie or crumble, served with cream from the farm down the lane and everyone says they couldn't possibly after all that roast beef, but then they agree that a little piece wouldn't do any harm and so they all tuck in.

Awfully nice blackcurrant pudding

This little dish is very easy and delicious and involves no cooking beyond a quick stewing of the blackcurrants. You can use any fruit — from apples to berries and stone fruits. But when blackcurrants are in season, this is for them. And you.

SERVES 4

Rinse the blackcurrants and tidy them up. Run a fork through each bunch to pull the berries from their stems. Set a few aside, just 2 or 3 berries per serving, then place the rest in a saucepan. Add the caster sugar and a scant tablespoonful of water and simmer gently for 10 minutes. When it's cool enough, check to see if you need a little more sugar — you should aim for a sweet but sharp flavour.

200g blackcurrants
50g caster sugar,
  plus more to taste
150ml double cream
150g vanilla yoghurt
demerara sugar,
  for sprinkling

Whip the cream in to soft peaks, then fold in the yoghurt. Divide the cooked blackcurrants between 4 ramekins, little dishes or even tumblers. Cover with the cream mixture and then smooth demerara sugar across the top of each one — how much really depends on your taste. Refrigerate for a good couple of hours. When you are ready to serve, dot with a few fresh blackcurrants.

Redcurrant relish

Redcurrants — sparkling glass beads of tart sweetness — are usually turned in to a jelly or relish and, as with so many products, home-made is much better, sharper, redder and fresher than anything you would buy in a shop.

To make a relish, give the redcurrants a good rinse and strip the berries from their stalks in to a pan using a fork. Add caster sugar to taste (be generous as the berries are tart), a splash of water and give the pan a bit of a shake before heating it all through slowly, just until the berries have flopped.

That's all. Pour it in to a pretty dish and serve alongside roast pork or lamb, oily fish, cheese and ham.

 Fresh from the bush or the farmers' market, redcurrants can also be used like pomegranate seeds, sprinkled over the top of salads, humous, couscous, granola and fruit salads, adding a bite and a shiver with their sharpness.

Stone fruit
Stoned love

I bite in to a ripe, white-fleshed peach, juice dripping down my chin, and I ask myself, 'Is one ever enough?' All the stone fruit roll in to season during the summer, starting with apricots, peaking with peaches and nectarines and ending with plums. OK, they can be a bit fiddly to eat, with the juice and the wasps and the what-to-do-with-the-stone situation, but it's all worth it for the variety of flavours, their endless versatility and unctuous sweetness when baked in the oven.

Fruit salads and crumbles really are just the beginning, because stone fruit can be quite easily and quickly transformed from summer fruit-bowl staples to sassy little numbers with hardly any fuss — as on the opposite page, with some crème fraîche and biscuits.

 Fruit, biscuit, cream

Halve any stone fruits, such as nectarines or apricots, and remove the stones. Place them, open side up, on a baking tray and generously sprinkle with brown sugar. Grill till golden and blackening around the edges, 5-10 minutes. Mix crème fraîche with some crumbled biscuits – Amaretti are especially good – and load this mixture on top of the fruit. Drizzle with honey or a sprinkle of caster sugar. Flash this back under a hot grill for a minute until the top is golden and bubbling. Allow to cool slightly and serve with more crème fraîche if needs be.

Grilled peaches with prosciutto, rocket and balsamic

Fresh, grilled, roasted or seared on a griddle, stone fruits work very well in salads, with cheeses such as feta and halloumi and with very finely sliced ham, especially prosciutto or Serrano. Mint, pine nuts, walnuts, almonds and toasted seeds are all happy to jump in to the mix and when you add a sweet dressing, you've got yourself a bit of a gathering.

SERVES 4

Put the peach halves, cut side down, on kitchen paper to dry for 5 minutes. Meanwhile, heat a griddle pan to a medium heat. Brush each peach half with sunflower oil and griddle them in batches, skin side down, for 2 minutes. Turn them over and griddle skin side uppermost for 1 minute.

Place the rocket and endive in a shallow bowl, mix the olive oil and vinegar together in a jug or jar and pour it over the salad leaves. Gently toss, then arrange the peach halves on top of the salad with the prosciutto and mozzarella. Finish with a grind of fresh black pepper.

4 peaches, halved and stoned
1 tbsp sunflower oil
140g rocket
1 head baby endive, trimmed
  and torn
2 tbsp olive oil
1 tbsp balsamic vinegar
12 slices of prosciutto ham
2 x 125g balls of buffalo
  mozzarella, torn in pieces

Cherry ripe

The British cherry, like so many of our formerly popular fruits, lost its foothold in the market for many years and for many reasons, becoming almost a rarity and an expensive one at that. But, with the development of more viable trees over recent years and the trend to eat more locally grown produce, it's making something of a comeback. So long as the weather doesn't play too many nasty tricks during the growing season, we can now afford to do more with them than share the odd bag or two.

Obviously, one of the best ways to eat them is straight out of the bag, spitting stones as you walk home until there's nothing left but a tell-tale trail. But, with more around and at better prices, I'm thinking jams and pies, I'm thinking sticky mixtures to spread inside chocolate cakes. I'm also thinking of some deeply darkly red cherry sauce — and, what do you know, here it is…

Sweet cherry spooning sauce

This is a deep purple, almost black, glossy, decadent sauce. Eat it cold or warm with yoghurt or spoon it hot over vanilla ice cream.

Combine all the ingredients in a bowl and leave them to steep for a minimum of 30 minutes. Pour the mixture in to a saucepan, put the lid on and allow it to simmer on the lowest possible heat for 30 minutes. Take the lid off and, keeping the heat very low, simmer for a further 15 minutes, until it is dark and unctuous.

*A cherry stoner is what you need for this job. They're not expensive and some can also be used for stoning olives.

500g cherries, stoned*
3 tbsp Maraschino liqueur
100g soft light brown sugar
half a cinnamon stick
1 tbsp runny honey

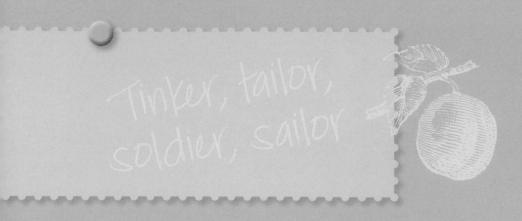

Tinker, tailor, soldier, sailor

Plums herald late summer in the garden and the kitchen and are a reminder, in case we need one, to make the most of the sunshine and its warmth while we can.

And eating a beautifully ripe plum straight from the tree is a moment to be treasured, apart from one thing — wasps. When I used to pick fruit as a child, the worst of all for wasps were plums. They have a knack of getting right inside and we would regularly be stung four or five times a day. So, even now, years later, there's a bit of a Russian roulette element to biting in to a plum for me.

Wasps aside, August is their month and, happily, plums — all sorts — are versatile. They can be turned in to pies and tarts, jams and chutneys, as well as being great for eating fresh from the tree, the grass or a brown paper bag.

And then there are damsons — tiny, dark little gems that are great in crumbles or just lightly stewed with plenty of sugar and the best for Tinker, Tailor, Soldier, Sailor, as children (well, everyone) can easily get to Thief — and some would even say Indian Chief — and back round again, with trails of little stones criss-crossing the supper table.

Plum frangipane

Use any variety of plum, though Victorias work very well for this flaky, almondy, sugar plum tart.

SERVES 6

Preheat the oven to 220°C/200°C fan/gas mark 7.

Roll the pastry in to a 26cm square (if you're using pre-rolled pastry then an oblong shape will do just as well) and place it on a non-stick baking sheet. Score a line all the way round 1.5cm from the edge, to form a rim. Prick the middle of the pastry several times, then place the tray in the oven. Bake for 5 minutes until the pastry starts to brown and rise. Remove from the oven and neatly press the centre down with the back of a spoon to ensure the rim is raised.

Cream the butter, 100g of the sugar and the orange zest together. Gradually beat in the eggs, making sure they are completely mixed in after each addition. Add the vanilla extract, then fold in the flour and the ground almonds. Tip this mixture on to the pastry base and smooth it out evenly, avoiding the rim.

Arrange the plum halves on top, cut sides down. Sprinkle with the remaining sugar and scatter with the flaked (or slivered) almonds. Return the tart to the oven, turn down the heat to 200°C/180°C fan/gas mark 6 and bake for 25 minutes, or until the fruit is soft and the almond mixture is risen and browned. Remove from the oven.

Melt the jam in a small saucepan, then brush it generously across the top of the tart to glaze it. Serve warm with a scoop of vanilla ice cream or a good spoonful of Greek yoghurt.

250g ready-made puff pastry
100g unsalted butter
150g caster sugar
the zest of half an orange
2 medium eggs, beaten
½ tsp vanilla extract
1 tbsp plain flour, sifted
100g ground almonds
330g ripe plums, halved and stoned
3 tbsp flaked or slivered almonds
3 tbsp plum jam

Elderflowers

An English summer's day in a glass

Foraging is a great idea in principle — getting out in to the fresh air to pick and gather edibles for nothing. But you have to know what you're looking for and what to do with your basketful of gatherings once you get home, you have to know where to look and find the time and, all in all, it's probably not going to happen that often for most of us.

Not so with elderflowers. They're everywhere — whether you're in the countryside or the middle of the town, there are going to be some flourishing on a scrap of land nearby. They're easily identified, quick and easy to pick and get home and then, when you do, you can make lovely summery elderflower cordial: frothy heads of delicately fragrant white flowers, steeped and poured in to bottles and then served in the garden on sunny days, from pretty jugs topped with lemon slices and ice — a ritual that is forever the English summertime at its best.

Elderflower etiquette requires that we don't strip trees bare, partly so there are some for other people to pick, but mostly so there are enough flowers turning to berries — for the birds and also for elderberry wine. More easy foraging.

Elderflower cordial

Do you make elderflower cordial? It's very satisfying, partly because the ratio of effort to praise is loaded in favour of praise and so you feel a bit chuffed, but mostly because you pick the main ingredient from a tree and that makes you feel you're down with nature, even if you're not usually. And something for nothing is always a bonus.

Citric acid can be bought at health food shops, at chemists and online, and is essentially there as an antioxidant. If you can't find any, just use the lemons, but the cordial probably won't keep as long.

MAKES ROUGHLY 1.5 LITRES

Carefully rinse the elderflower heads to clean them and check for bugs. Set them aside and find a bowl large enough to hold all the ingredients.

Tip the sugar in to the bowl, pour in the boiling water and stir. Leave to cool for a good half hour before adding the citric acid, lemon slices and finally the elderflower heads.

Cover the bowl with a tea towel and leave the mix in a cool place to infuse for 24 hours. Strain through some muslin and carefully pour in to washed, sterilized bottles. Store in the fridge where it should keep for 3-4 weeks.

When you're ready to drink the cordial, pour some in a jug and add water — still or fizzy — to taste. Add lemon slices and ice and then, if you like, mint leaves, lemon balm, borage flowers — whatever is in the garden and looks like it ought to feature. A clinking jug on a summer's day is always a moment to celebrate.

30 freshly picked elderflower heads, no brown tips
1.5kg caster sugar
1.2l boiling water
75g citric acid
3 lemons, sliced

•••

To sterilize jars, wash them in hot soapy water, rinse and shake off the excess water. Put them on a baking tray in a low oven for 10 minutes. Alternatively, you can run them through a hot wash in a dishwasher.

•••

Elderflower and gooseberry crumble cake with elderflower cream

Peaking in July, gooseberries have a bit of a blink-and-you've-missed-them season, which probably explains why they aren't as popular as they ought to be – people just don't get round to trying them, which is a shame, because they are so well suited to traditional British puddings like syllabubs and fools.

They have a real affinity with elderflowers, coming from that same aromatic/floral arc of the taste spectrum. This cake, more of a pudding really, celebrates and combines both flavours to perfection and is good served either warm or cold. Any variety of gooseberry will do – pink, red, yellow or green – whichever kind you can lay your hands on.

SERVES 6

Preheat the oven to 190°C/170°C fan/gas mark 5, then lightly butter a loose-bottomed cake tin 20cm in diameter and line with baking parchment.

Top and tail the gooseberries, mix with the caster sugar and 2 tablespoons of cordial and set aside. If you have found pink or red gooseberries, hold a spoonful back to put on the top at the end as a garnish.

Cream the butter and brown sugar together, then slowly add the eggs, beating as you go. Beat in the remaining tablespoon of cordial and fold in the flour. Transfer the cake mixture to the tin and spread the gooseberries on top.

To make the crumble, cream the butter and sugar together, then incorporate the flour so you get a good knobbly mix. Alternatively, place all the crumble topping ingredients in a food processor and whizz for 20 seconds.

Scatter the crumble topping over the gooseberries and sprinkle with a tablespoon of water. Bake for an hour or so, until the crumble is cooked and the fruit is tender. You may want to lightly cover it with foil halfway through if you think the top is browning too quickly. Allow the cake to cool in the tin for a good half hour, before carefully transferring to a wire rack.

To make the elderflower cream, whip the cream until it's good and thick, then slowly add the cordial, drop by drop, beating a little as you go to keep the cream thick.

FOR THE CAKE
350g gooseberries
110g caster sugar
3 tbsp elderflower cordial
110g butter, softened
1 tbsp brown sugar
2 large eggs, beaten
175g self-raising flour, sifted

FOR THE CRUMBLE TOPPING
75g butter
75g caster sugar
110g self-raising flour

FOR THE ELDERFLOWER CREAM
140ml double cream
1 tbsp elderflower cordial

Drinks and smoothies

The summer months are a fantastic time to mix it up on the drinks front as there is so much to choose from. Berries, currants and stone fruits can all be blended for fresh juices. Mint, elderflower, lavender and rosewater add the quintessential scents and flavours of an English summer. Then you just need some pretty glasses and sunshine to get blending, stirring and out in to the garden with a trayful of colourful drinks.

Be careful about putting ice in your blender, though. Most domestic blenders are fine with crushed ice, but not with ice cubes. If you don't have any crushed ice, get a sturdy plastic bag and a rolling pin and bash the ice cubes in to smaller pieces.

Kir royale

Classically, 1 part crème de cassis to 4 parts champagne, but sparkling wine can also be used to make this celebratory cocktail. Serve it with the pavlova on page 110, the birthday cake on page 113, as drinks on the terrace, at summer parties and for anything involving adults and balloons.

Strawberry and elderflower cooler

As with the peach, raspberry and vanilla drink, you can also add some fizz — alcoholic or non — to this mixture, to turn it in to a summer cocktail.

MAKES 2 TALL GLASSES

Blend all the ingredients together. Once smooth, pour in tall glasses, each with their own strawberry cut almost in half and perched over the rim.

250g strawberries
75ml elderflower cordial
100ml fresh orange juice,
   or the juice of 1-2 oranges
a couple of handfuls
   of crushed ice

Peach, raspberry and vanilla fizz

Very good for a summer lunch party. If you are making this for a special occasion you can substitute champagne or sparkling wine for the fizzy water. If you can find white-fleshed peaches, so much the better, but yellow peaches and nectarines make good alternatives.

MAKES 2 TALL GLASSES

Put the peaches, raspberries (thawed if using frozen) and vanilla extract in the blender and whizz together with about one tablespoon of caster sugar — it all depends on the sweetness of the peaches. If you like, you can then put the pureé through a sieve to remove the raspberry pips.

Pour in tall glasses and add fizzy water to taste, stirring to combine. You can continue to top up with the water if you like, slowly turning this from a fruity drink with some fizz to a fizzy drink with some fruit.

2 ripe and juicy
  peaches, skinned,
  stoned and chopped
100g raspberries,
  fresh or frozen
1 tsp vanilla extract
caster sugar, to taste
500ml chilled fizzy water

Tropical milkshake

A very sexy drink, good for the late afternoon or early evening. It's possible that grown-ups might even drizzle a shot of rum in to their glass at the last minute.

MAKES 4 TALL GLASSES

Put the coconut milk, pineapple juice, mango, lime zest and juice and crushed ice in the blender and blend until smooth. Taste for sweetness and add some honey if you think it's needed.

Pour in tall glasses, add a scoop of vanilla ice cream to each one and squeeze the juice and pulp from the passion fruit halves on top. Serve with stripy straws and paper umbrellas if you have them.

1 x 400ml tin of
  coconut milk
250ml fresh pineapple juice
1 large fresh mango, peeled
  and roughly chopped
the zest and juice of 2 limes
a couple of handfuls of
  crushed ice
honey (optional)

TO SERVE
4 scoops of vanilla ice cream
2 passion fruit, halved

Ooh, you big smoothie!

It's a very fruity time of year and, when everything is at such good prices, it's tempting to buy too much and, before you know it, the fruit flies are hovering. Good job, then, for smoothies, the great catch-all for fruit about to turn. The possibilities are endless. Normally, a smoothie includes banana, but not always. The more banana, the thicker it will be and, obviously, the stronger the banana flavour too.

Some fruits lend themselves better than others to the smoothie experience. During the summer, strawberries and raspberries are good. So are peaches and nectarines. Pears and apples are better if they've been roasted first to break them down, though a pear that's turned overnight (like they sneakily do) is ready for the big whizz.

Experiment with flavours and textures. Try adding cinnamon along with apples and pears, vanilla extract, honey, oats or wheatgerm, a splash of cordial, a shot of coffee, cocoa powder, ice cream… the thinking being that sometimes a smoothie should be a bolt of health-giving goodness, and other times just a treat and to hell with healthy.

Melon and ginger smoothie

Different melons give different colours and subtle differences in flavour too. Cantaloupes, for example, with their orange flesh, make a gorgeous peachy-coloured smoothie when mixed

with yoghurt. This is a good drink to make with a melon that's heading towards over-ripe. The quantities here are just a guide, as it all depends how ripe the melon is, so you'll have to feel your way through till you get the right consistency. Same with the honey, bunny.

MAKES 4 SMALL GLASSES

1 medium melon
1 thumbnail of fresh ginger
250g plain yoghurt
the juice of 1 lemon
1 tbsp honey, or more to taste

Quarter the melon, peel and deseed, then cut the flesh in chunks. Peel and finely chop the ginger. Place them in the blender with all the other ingredients. Blitz. Taste to check how sweet the smoothie is and add more honey if needed.

Avocado, lime and apple shots

Almost a mousse, the texture is silky smooth, the colour is delicate, the taste is classy and delicious.

MAKES 4 SMALL GLASSES

Halve the avocado, which should be just ripe or even slightly unripe, remove the stone and scoop the flesh in to the blender. Add the other ingredients and blitz until smooth. Serve in delicate Moroccan tea glasses if you have them.

1 Hass avocado
175ml fresh apple juice
2 tbsp lime juice
2 tsp caster sugar

Strawberry, elderflower and yoghurt smoothie

Not just a smoothie — you can also freeze this mixture in lolly moulds to make creamy, healthy, summery treats.

MAKES 2 TALL GLASSES

250g strawberries, plus
  more to decorate
250g Greek or plain
  yoghurt
4 tbsp elderflower cordial
a handful of crushed ice
  (optional)

Rinse and hull the strawberries, then place all the ingredients in the blender and blitz. Pour in glasses and decorate with a strawberry or two.

Lunch in the garden

As you will have gathered by now, I'm a great fan of eating outside, of grabbing a few essentials and heading off: to a corner of the garden, the park, a hill, the beach. It might be just you and an apple or a whole gathering, involving cars and kids, cool bags and cricket bats. The point is, so far as the food is concerned, you should be looking for grab-and-go dishes that can quickly be slipped on to a plate or in to a few bags, then it's off and out of the house in no time.

Sandwiches are the obvious choice — fresh bread sliced, filled and wrapped in minutes. Big salads are another good call, especially when you're covering all the essentials in one dish that can easily be spooned in to bowls — like a chicken Caesar salad or, say, a blue cheese, walnuts and figs combination. Plenty of healthy and fresh ingredients in one container is what you want, rather than lots of fiddly plastic tubs containing different bits and pieces.

When I was growing up, salad wasn't the soul-stirring feast of colour, texture and flavour that we eat nowadays. Celery sticks were stuffed in a jug, there was a plate of tomato quarters, another plate with a cucumber on it and some lettuce, maybe some cress and radishes, a bowl of sliced beetroot in vinegar. The salad cream was the best bit, poured like gravy over the whole lot. I know children can be reluctant salad eaters, but in those days so were the adults.

But then, along came a glamorous person from a glossy magazine who pointed her long red fingernail at those lost ingredients, went away to get some stylish accessories and then came back to carry out the most creative and gob-smacking before-and-after makeover of her career. Salad had thrown away her sensible shoes and was ready to party.

There really are very few rules, and even those are there for the breaking in the name of texture, flavour and colour. Experiment and mix it up, never more so than during the summer months, when everything is fresh and zesty and at its, er, besty.

Melon, prosciutto and Pecorino with a chilli dressing

For high summer, when beautifully ripe melons are plentiful and you're looking for something quick and light for lunch.

You can use just one type of melon or a mix if that's what you have. Likewise with the Pecorino, you can substitute Parmesan.

SERVES 4

Cut the melon in crescents or bite-sized chunks and arrange them in a shallow dish. Lay the ham on top and scatter with the cheese. Mix the dressing ingredients together and season to taste, then spoon this across and finish with the basil leaves.

1 melon
4 thin slices of prosciutto ham
100g Pecorino cheese shavings
a handful of basil leaves, torn

FOR THE DRESSING
4 tbsp olive oil
2 tbsp balsamic vinegar
1 small red chilli, deseeded
  and finely chopped

Grilled salmon with new potatoes and beetroot

A flavoursome dish that can be plated up for lunch in the garden or layered in a container for a picnic and assembled on the spot. Classy, but carefree at the same time.

SERVES 4

Preheat the oven to 200°C/180°C fan/gas mark 6.

In a large dish, mix together the lime zest and juice and the olive oil. Add the salmon fillets, make sure they are well coated in the marinade and leave for an hour.

Meanwhile, wash the beetroot and wrap each one in foil. Place on a baking tray and bake for 45 minutes, or until just tender. Leave to cool for 30 minutes, then peel and cut in bite-sized chunks.

Wash the potatoes, halve the larger ones and keep the smaller ones whole. Place them in a large pan of boiling, salted water and cook for 10 minutes, or until just tender. Drain and set aside.

Preheat the grill to the highest setting.

To prepare the dressing, mix all the ingredients together in a small bowl. Season with salt and freshly ground black pepper.

Add the beetroot, potatoes and rocket or mixed baby salad leaves to a large salad bowl. Pour over the dressing and gently toss together.

Put the salmon fillets skin side up on a baking tray and season with salt and freshly ground black pepper. Place under the hot grill and cook for 3-6 minutes, depending on thickness – the skin should be crispy and the flesh pale pink.

To serve, divide the salad between the plates, top with a salmon fillet and garnish with the amaranth or spinach leaves.

the zest and juice of 1 lime
2 tbsp olive oil
4 salmon fillets, roughly 150g each
3 medium beetroot (approx. 300g)
400g Jersey Royal or other new potatoes
140g rocket or mixed baby salad leaves
a handful of red amaranth leaves or spinach leaves

FOR THE DRESSING
6 tbsp crème fraîche
1 tbsp horseradish sauce
a good handful of fresh dill, finely chopped
1 tbsp white wine vinegar
1 tbsp olive oil

Bill's chicken Caesar salad

What you're aiming for with this salad is the sort of dish you can shovel in to your mouth, great forkfuls of flavour, while lying on the sofa watching the box or lolling in a hammock — horizontal food. That's not to say that's necessarily how you'll be eating it, but it's good to have the option. It's also great picnic food as it can stand a bit of jostling.

SERVES 6-8

Preheat the oven to 180°C/160°C fan/gas mark 4.

Place the chicken in a baking tray or roasting tin. Cut the lemon in half and place it in the cavity along with the garlic bulb halves. Rub the chicken with the olive oil and a good sprinkle of sea salt. Put the chicken in the oven and cook for 30 minutes before removing.

Tear the bread in rough, bite-sized pieces and put them in and around the chicken with the pancetta and rosemary. Return the chicken to the oven.

After about 10 minutes, once the pancetta has started to cook, use the back of a fork to really squish the croutons in to the juices. Toss them around a bit several times and squish them in to the juices again, then drizzle half the stock over them. The idea here is, frankly, to create probably the best croutons you've ever tasted.

Cook for another 45-50 minutes, until the chicken is cooked through, adding more stock to the croutons if you think they need it. They should be chewy/crispy rather than just crispy, or even burnt, offerings.

Remove the chicken dish from the oven and allow to cool for 20 minutes or so. Keep the roasted garlic cloves and squeeze them in to the salad if you like it extra garlicky, or use them spread on bruschetta.

1 x 1.6kg free-range chicken
1 lemon
1 whole bulb of garlic, cut
  in half across the middle
3 tbsp olive oil
250g white bread
70g pancetta, cut in cubes
6 sprigs of rosemary
100ml chicken stock
1 large cos lettuce, torn
  in bite-sized pieces
100g Parmesan shavings

FOR THE DRESSING
half an onion, diced
half a bulb of fennel,
  cut in small dice
1 garlic clove
1 tsp Dijon mustard
the juice of half a lemon
1½ tsp sherry vinegar
285ml olive oil
75g Parmesan, grated
1 anchovy fillet

Meanwhile, make the dressing: place the onion, fennel and garlic in a blender and blitz together. Add the mustard, lemon juice and vinegar and keep blending. Slowly add the olive oil and grated Parmesan. Finally add the anchovy fillet, season and give one final blitz to create a smooth cream.

When you are ready to assemble the salad, tear the chicken apart — you are aiming for rustic rather than tidy pieces. Place the lettuce, chicken, pancetta, rosemary, Parmesan shavings and croutons in a large shallow bowl. Pour the dressing over and, using either two wooden spoons or clean hands, gently lift and fold everything together so that each potential mouthful is packed with flavour, each piece of chicken and lettuce dotted with Parmesan and covered with unctuous dressing. Serve generously.

Goat's cheese and roast beetroot salad

Sweet, caramelized onions, the big purple flavour of beetroot, the sharpness of goat's cheese —
lovely flavours finished with a creamy dressing.

SERVES 4

Preheat the oven to 180°C/160°C fan/gas mark 4.

Wrap each beetroot loosely in foil and roast in the oven for
30-40 minutes, until cooked through. Set aside to cool
for a while before peeling them.

Meanwhile, heat 2 tablespoons of olive oil in a large frying
pan and cook the onion with a pinch of salt over a medium
heat for 10 minutes. Add the sugar and butter and cook
for a further 2 minutes until soft and gently caramelized.
Tip the onions on to kitchen paper to absorb any excess oil
and leave to cool for 10 minutes.

Quarter each cooled beetroot and then cut each quarter
in half again. Combine the remaining olive oil with
the sherry vinegar and a good sprinkle of salt, add the
beetroot and mix well to coat in the dressing. Set aside.

Place a good handful of leaves — I like a combination of baby
spinach, rocket and little gem lettuce — on each plate.
Mix the mascarpone and horseradish in a small bowl, then
spoon over each salad. Pile the beetroot on top, followed by
the onions. Finish with a slice of goat's cheese, a sprinkle of
chopped parsley or some amaranth leaves if you have some,
and a good twist of black pepper.

4 medium beetroot
 (approx. 400g)
4 tbsp olive oil
1 large onion, sliced
½ tsp sugar
½ tsp butter
2 tbsp sherry vinegar
70g mixed leaves
4 tbsp mascarpone cheese
1½ tsp horseradish sauce
120g log of goat's cheese,
 cut in 4 slices
a handful of parsley,
 finely chopped (optional)
red amaranth leaves,
 to garnish (optional)

Fire, cook, eat

Barbecues

I started this summer section with a big thumbs-up to us all for giving it a go even when the good weather forgets to turn up for the party. And so it is only fair that we devote a page or two to that most beloved and unpredictable affair – the barbecue. Let's not even get in to why we do it. We just do.

There are some very good things about barbecues and there are some very bad things about them too. If we start with the bad, I would kick off with paper plates. And cups. And, at its worst, plastic cutlery. How and when did that ever happen?

Next would have to be the concept that a barbecue means a meat feast and the unspoken agreement that everyone must have a lamb chop, a burger, a sausage, a piece of chicken. Finally, there's the idea that it needs to involve an awful lot of dishes of all sorts and so somehow it also becomes a picnic and a buffet and, well, a bit of a mess.

BUT, a good barbecue knocks all that lot in to a cocked hat. When the location is right, the weather doesn't let us down, the food is simple and full of flavour – and not burnt – a barbecue is one of the very best ways to eat outdoors.

The main trick, in my opinion, is not to get too fancy. What works, what keeps things calm, is a couple of big hitters on the barbie, one very good salad, a few nice extras, like relishes and pouring sauces, and plenty of good bread. You also need some treats for people to pick at while the food is cooking on the barbecue, something sweet to eat afterwards and plenty to drink.

That way, what started out as somebody's very good idea to head off to the beach and cook a few sausages can stay as that, instead of it turning in to preparations similar to those undertaken by hardy explorers setting off to discover the New World.

So, what to cook? I do think it's hard to beat a top-quality chorizo sausage in a bun – juicy and flavoursome, packed in some decent bread with a few leaves, it's almost criminally good. And halloumi comes in to its own when seared on a barbecue – salty, chewy and blackened, mixed with some leaves and drizzled with a spiky sweet chilli sauce, it becomes another contender for the courthouse.

To roast peppers, start by quartering and deseeding them. Slice (thinly or in chunks, as the recipe requires) and put in a bowl. Lightly coat in olive oil and then scatter the pieces on a baking tray. Roast in a preheated oven (200°C/180°C fan/gas mark 6) for up to 30 minutes, until softened and somewhat blackened. If you like you can slip the skins off, which is much easier to do once they're roasted.

Hot chorizo sandwich

This has got to be up there as a front-runner for all-time golden foodie moment.

MAKES 6

Take 2 slices of just-griddled sourdough, spread with a tablespoon of humous and fill with a very good chorizo sausage straight off the barbecue, a few roasted peppers — maybe whacked on to the barbecue for the last few minutes — and a handful of rocket leaves, the whole lot drizzled with some peppery olive oil. Try not to drool while doing this and then find a quiet place to sit and savour the moment and your sandwich.

12 slices of sourdough
6 tbsp ready-made or
  home-made humous
  (see recipe on page 279)
6 large chorizo sausages,
  grilled or barbecued
2 red peppers, sliced in chunks
  and roasted or griddled
a good handful of rocket leaves
olive oil, for drizzling

Halloumi burgers

Salty and textured, halloumi is a really good fridge stalwart, lifting the
ordinary to soul-satisfying in a few minutes of dry frying. And if you're
happy with a bit of multi-tasking on the barbecue front, you can cook
the halloumi for these burgers in a frying pan on a corner of the barbecue
rather than nipping back and forth to the kitchen.

MAKES 6

Cut the halloumi in finger-width slices and slowly dry-fry
in a frying pan over the barbecue until golden, flipping them
over to do both sides. Meanwhile, briefly griddle the roasted
pepper slices. Grill the sourdough by deftly pushing each slice
down on to the barbecue griddles. Then make big sandwiches
filled with halloumi, onions, peppers, humous and rocket,
drizzled generously with olive oil and sweet chilli sauce.

300g halloumi
2 red peppers, sliced and roasted
12 slices of sourdough
2 onions, finely sliced and fried
6 tbsp ready-made or home-made humous
  (see recipe on page 279)
a good handful of rocket leaves
olive oil and sweet chilli sauce,
  for drizzling

Two good dishes for serving alongside or inside burgers

Quick summer beans

SERVES 4–6

Put the runner beans — or any other green beans that are cheap and plentiful — and red onion in a large bowl. Combine the dressing ingredients and fold in to the vegetables, then season with salt and freshly ground black pepper.

225g runner beans, finely sliced
1 small red onion, finely sliced

FOR THE DRESSING
100ml crème fraîche
2 tsp lemon juice
1 tbsp wholegrain mustard
½ tsp honey

Mango salsa

As well as being great for adding to any type of burger, this is also good for serving alongside curries.

MAKES 1 LARGE BOWLFUL

Put the mango chutney in a bowl and add the coriander, chilli, sweet chilli sauce, onion and lime juice. Mix thoroughly, then fold in the fresh mango and nigella seeds.

170g mango chutney
4 heaped tbsp finely chopped
   fresh coriander
1 red chilli, deseeded and
   finely diced
1 tbsp sweet chilli sauce
1 small red onion, finely chopped
the juice of half a lime
1 large ripe mango, peeled and
   finely diced
1 tsp nigella seeds

Brownies and blondies

On a perfect day, when the sun shines and nobody grazes their knee or gets stung or loses their car keys in the pebbles, when there are loos quite nearby and nobody gets lost and the person who normally irritates everyone doesn't, what you need to complete the all-round perfectness is somebody to produce a battered tin containing layer upon layer of something home-made and sweet and preferably chocolatey.

Here you go, then. Your turn to experience the warm glow of being ever so slightly saintly as you pass around gooey more-ish brownies and deliciously rich blondies.

Bill's brownies

Very chocolatey, very nutty, delicious and essential. If you like you can vary the nuts —
Brazil nuts or macadamias are also very good in these brownies.

Preheat the oven to 180°C/160°C fan/gas mark 4
and lightly butter a 24 x 33cm baking tin.

Spread the nuts over a baking tray and toast them in
the oven for about 4 minutes. Keep an eye on things,
as they can burn quickly. Remove the tray from the
oven, let the nuts cool and then roughly chop them.

Gently melt the chocolate and butter together in a
bowl sitting over a pan of simmering water, stirring
occasionally, then take them off the heat and add
the coffee and vanilla extract. Beat the mixture until
it is glossy and smooth, Scrape in to a large bowl
and set aside to cool slightly.

In another large bowl, whisk together the eggs and
sugar for about 5 minutes until pale and thick.
Slowly fold the egg mixture in to the warm chocolate.

Sieve the flour and cocoa powder together, add the salt,
then gently fold this in to the chocolate mixture. Finally,
stir in the nuts, distributing them well but being
careful not to over-mix.

Pour the brownie mixture in to the dish and bake for
20-25 minutes or so, until the top has that classic pale
and sheeny finish. Make sure not to overcook, as you
still want a gooey inside.

Cool for 15 minutes, cut in to squares, remove from the
tin and when they're completely cool, pack them ready for
your picnic.

55g pecan nuts
55g hazelnuts
55g almonds
200g 70% dark chocolate,
  roughly chopped or broken
250g butter
2 tsp instant coffee granules
½ tsp vanilla extract
4 large eggs
250g muscovado sugar
90g plain flour
15g cocoa powder
½ tsp fine sea salt

Bill's blondies

You don't need me to talk you through why you should make these. Just look at the ingredients. I will say cut them small because they're quite rich, and make sure you're not left with too many because you *will* eat them all.

MAKES 16 SMALL SQUARES

Preheat the oven to 170°C/150°C fan/gas mark 3 and line a 20 x 20cm (or equivalent capacity) baking tray with baking parchment.

Melt the butter in a pan over a low heat, then add the chocolate and continue to heat gently, stirring occasionally, until melted together. Remove the pan from the heat, stir in the vanilla extract and lemon zest and leave to cool slightly.

Put the eggs and sugar in a large bowl and whisk until the mixture thickens. Gently fold in the flour and, when that is nicely mixed in, fold through the cherries, apricots and biscuit pieces. Finally, slowly add the chocolate mixture and combine everything well.

Pour in to the lined tray and bake for 35-40 minutes or until firm and pale gold on top. Cut in squares while still warm, but leave in the tray until completely cool before removing.

125g unsalted butter
200g white chocolate,
  chopped in small pieces
1 tsp vanilla extract
the zest of half a lemon
2 large eggs, beaten
100g caster sugar
130g plain flour, sifted
100g glacé cherries, quartered
100g dried apricots,
  chopped in small pieces
4 ginger biscuits,
  broken in pieces

And so it comes to pass that your moment of domestic saintliness is over, the cake tin is empty, the fire is down to the embers and it's time to pack up and head home. There's a chill in the air and it's getting darker that bit earlier. Yes, we have to face it and then embrace it: we're heading towards autumn.

AUTUMN.

Bringing Home the Bounty

There's something about the way summer slips in to autumn that can take your breath away, with nature slowly winding things down and delivering some of the year's best produce as she goes.

Add to that the children going back to school, the crispness in the air each morning, the leaves turning and the football season getting in to full swing, and although it's a sign we're heading towards winter, there's also a sense of good things to come. Throw in the smell of wood smoke and I'll be needing someone to tell me to pull myself together.

And there really are good things to come. This is the season that brings home the bounty and would once have been the time when store cupboards were overflowing with jars of jams and pickles, boxes of fruit wrapped and packed in to dark corners, strings of onions and bottles of wine. Today we can enjoy the glow of all that domesticity without the strain of making sure there's still something left in the larder come springtime.

And just as the season slowly mellows from summer to autumn, so does the produce. Plums, figs, blackberries and sweetcorn all mark soft September days as much as the tail-end of August, bringing some late summer warmth on to the table for as long as possible.

Then in come the autumn big hitters — apples and pears, squash and pumpkins, mushrooms and nuts. These guys are definitely the godfathers of the food world. They don't stand for any nonsense, muscling in with their big flavours and their chuck-anything-at-me-cos-I-can-take-it attitude. Every season's produce feels right for the time, but none more so than now. Great big robust dishes are what we're needing — soups and risottos, pies and puddings — warming dishes to cheer us through, and here we have, right on cue, a perfect batch of flavours and textures to do just that.

So, let rip with falling leaves and shorter days, blast us with cold snaps. We're ready, with the fire alight, plenty in the store cupboard and good food on the table.

Bill's

AUTUMN CHAMPIONS

As the weather turns, autumn unleashes a glory of delicious vegetables
and fruit to warm and comfort through colder days.

Plenty for everyone

Bill's autumn champion

Sweetcorn
Butterfingers

Children may turn up their noses at many vegetables, but one thing most of them will go for is a fat, sweet, juicy corn cob. The high sugar content, the sensation of the kernels bursting and tumbling in to their mouths, the no-cutlery-required way in which they can get stuck in all mean that a buttery corn cob just has to be a winner.

A staple in many parts of the world, eaten fresh, dried and ground in to meal, used to make everything from tamales to bread and oil, corn kernels can be used in fritters and added to salads, soups and chowders — but for me the pleasure is in eating them just as they are and as often as possible during their short and sweet season which spans late summer and the early part of autumn.

SO, TWO WAYS TO COOK THEM:

1. Strip off the husks, tidy them up and cook in boiling water for 5 minutes. Drain and coat with butter. A good sprinkle of sea salt (and some freshly ground black pepper if you like) and you're good to go.

2. Place them, still wrapped in their husks, on the barbecue. Keep cooking and turning them till they're blackened. Remove the husks and put the cobs back on the barbecue for a few more minutes.

Some kernels of sweetcorn advice

Choose cobs that are full and plump, with a good, tight wrapping of fresh green husk and silky threads (sweetcorn's a strange-looking beast when you think about it...). If the cobs don't have husks, the creamier the colour of the kernels, the fresher they are.

The natural sugars in sweetcorn start to turn in to starch very quickly after picking, particularly in warm weather. So refrigerate the cobs the moment you get them home and eat them as soon as possible to enjoy them at their sweetest freshest best. If you're not planning to eat them for a couple of days, blanch the cobs for a minute in boiling water and refresh in ice cold water before you refrigerate them, as this slows down the starch process and keeps them sweeter for longer.

If you want smaller pieces, snap cobs in half before cooking as it's much easier than after.

Mushrooms

From the field to your plate

It's mushroom season. Out in the woods and fields they're growing away, as the cool damp weather provides just the conditions they love, and so it's time for some early-morning mushrooming. You do have to know what you're doing, though. I've been picking mushrooms for years and even I'm still a bit nervous. So, if you're not sure, the best thing to do is go picking with someone who really knows their mushroom stuff.

Whether you've been skipping through the fields or down the supermarket aisles, once you get your seasonal mushrooms home, don't wash them. Just brush them gently with a dry pastry brush and then wipe with a clean, damp cloth to remove any dirt. When they're clean, how you cook them is up to you, though for me a poached egg and a few rashers of bacon are likely to feature. Some people like simply to fry them and eat them on their own, but I like to mix up the flavours to bring out the flavours, if you know what I mean.

Blue cheese sits very happily with mushrooms. Melt some butter in a pan and when it's hot, throw in some broken mushrooms. Fry for 3 minutes, then tip them, juices and all, on to some hot buttered toast. Crumble blue cheese across the top, add chopped parsley, if you have any, and season well.

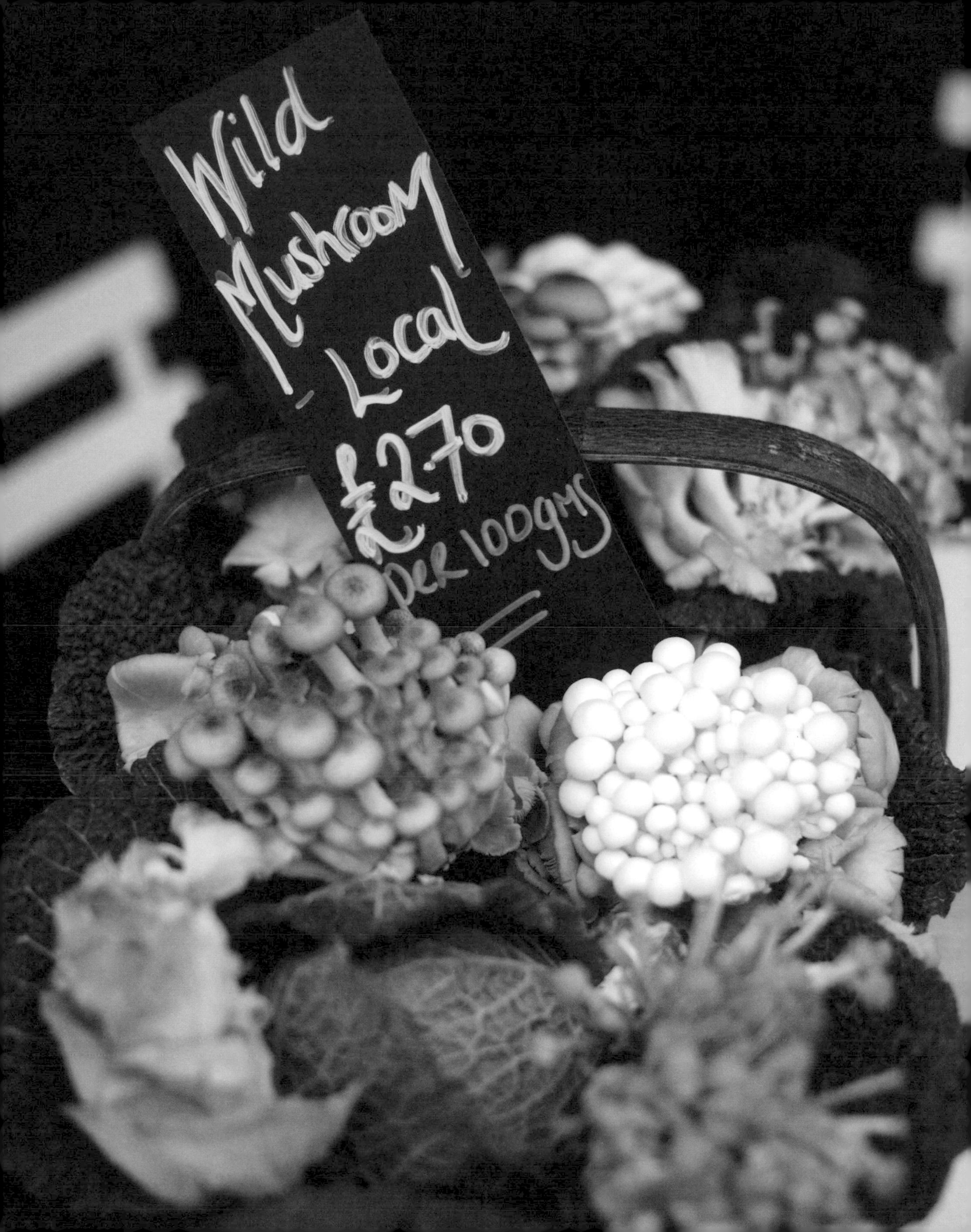
Wild
Mushroom
Local
£2.70
per 100gms

Mushroom and leek quiche

A real feast of a quiche, this one, packed with mushrooms. Go for a mix including oyster, button, shiitake, cep, chestnut, bluett or even truffle shavings.

SERVES 4–6

To make the pastry, sift the flour in to a large bowl and add the butter. Rub them together lightly with your fingertips to form a breadcrumb-like mixture, then add enough egg to bring the dough together. Add the herbs and a pinch of salt, and quickly knead to form a smooth dough. Form in a ball, wrap in cling film and chill in the fridge for 30 minutes.

Preheat the oven to 200°C/180°C fan/gas mark 6, then lightly butter a 23cm diameter flan tin and line it with baking parchment.

Roll out the pastry and carefully lift and press it in to the flan tin, line with baking parchment and baking beans and blind bake for 15 minutes. Remove from the oven, take out the beans and paper, and return to the oven for 5 more minutes until the pastry is golden brown.

While the pastry is baking, heat the butter in a large pan. When it's hot, add the leeks and cook them gently till they're soft. Tip them in a bowl and set aside. Put the olive oil in the pan, turn the heat up and add the garlic and mushrooms, adding larger, meatier ones first and tiny ones towards the end. Quickly fry the mushrooms until they are golden brown. Take the pan off the heat and add the leeks, straining off any liquid first. Stir in the sage, horseradish and half the pine nuts, then put this pan to one side.

Toast the remaining pine nuts by dry-frying them in a small frying pan until they start to turn golden (keep an eye on them as they can burn in a moment), then leave to cool.

Spread the chutney over the base of the pastry case. Drain away any liquid from the mushrooms and leeks again, then spoon them on top. Beat the cream, milk and eggs together in a jug or bowl and pour over the mushrooms and leeks. Sprinkle with the toasted pine nuts and a dusting of nutmeg. Bake at 200°C/180°C fan/gas mark 6 for 20–25 minutes, or until the tart is set and golden on top. Leave to cool in the tin for 5–10 minutes.

Serve with a simple green salad or try the coleslaw on page 264 or any of the autumn salads starting on page 200.

FOR THE PASTRY
200g plain flour
100g salted butter, chilled and cubed
1 medium egg, beaten
2 good pinches of dried mixed herbs

FOR THE FILLING
25g unsalted butter
2 leeks, finely sliced
2 tbsp olive oil
2 garlic cloves, finely chopped
500g mushrooms, big ones sliced and small ones left whole
2 sprigs of fresh sage, finely chopped
1 tsp horseradish sauce
2 tbsp pine nuts
2 tbsp chutney
125ml double cream
125ml milk
2 large eggs, beaten
a pinch of ground nutmeg

Leeks

Call for the kitchen cavalry

Great team players, leeks. They can sit quietly in the background, adding flavour and depth to a whole range of dishes, or they can be the main event. They don't mind how you cook them — though they seem to love butter best — and can be griddled, roasted or braised in the oven, stir-fried, sautéed, steamed or grilled.

If they're small and slender, you can eat them raw, sliced very finely and either mixed with other raw vegetables or on their own folded through a creamy mustard dressing. Larger leeks are the mainstay of many a dish and, like onions, they work with huge numbers of textures and flavours, but are particularly good with chicken, in rich unctuous stews, with tomatoes and with cheese.

They add depth to a risotto, work very well with pasta and are as happy wrapped in a cheese sauce or buttery pastry — or both — as a squirrel gathering nuts. What's more, as vegetable gardeners will tell you, leeks are very easy to grow and will cheerfully sit in the ground long after they've matured, ready for you to nip out and grab one or two when you need them.

Bill's cock-a-leekie

This is a chicken-free version of the classic dish, so less cock-a-leekie than simple leekie. It's a very good soup for autumn, the slow cooking of the vegetables and the addition of prunes giving it a warmth and richness that get right to the heart of comfort cooking.

SERVES 4

Heat the oil in a large pan and gently fry the onion for 5 minutes till translucent. Add the butter, and when it's melted and bubbling, tip in half the leeks, potatoes, celery and the sage, setting aside a few leaves for garnish. Cook gently for 25 minutes over a low heat with the lid on, stirring from time to time.

Add the stock to the vegetables and simmer for 10 minutes, then take off the heat and allow to cool slightly before briefly blitzing in a food processor until smooth.

Return the soup to the pan, add the remaining chopped vegetables and the honey, then season to taste. Replace the lid and simmer for a further 10–15 minutes, or until the vegetables are tender. Chop the prunes and add them for the last 5 minutes.

Garnish each bowl of soup with a couple of fresh sage leaves and serve with some good crusty bread.

1 tbsp olive oil
1 small onion, diced
1 tbsp butter
2 large or 3 medium leeks, cleaned and diced
4 medium potatoes (approx. 450g), peeled and diced
2–3 sticks of celery, diced
a small bunch of fresh sage, finely chopped, plus extra for garnishing
1 litre hot vegetable stock
1 tbsp honey
75g pitted soft prunes

Leek and Cheddar buck rarebit

There comes a time, during the autumn, for football — playing it, watching it, reading about it, listening to pundits discussing it — the beautiful game has many highlights and one of them is Saturday afternoon, when a gathering together of friends is likely to feature, and if it's all round to your house, you'll need some staples that extend beyond a crate of beer.

Without question, these staples should be of the big-savoury-hit variety, partly to soak up the beer and partly, if you've been running around on a pitch all afternoon, because you'll be needing it.

Home-made burgers stuffed in a bun are good, served alongside a tray of golden oven chips made from roughly chopped potatoes, skins on, tossed in some olive oil and sea salt and cooked in a hottish oven for about an hour. Pizza is also good, as are sausages, oven-baked and sandwiched between pieces of toasted sourdough or with a helping of creamy mash. But this is different. And it's also easy: buck rarebit, with the addition of some leeks. A very Welsh Welsh rarebit!

You can add ham, grilled mushrooms or flaked mackerel to your rarebit too if you fancy it. If you do, the extra ingredients go on to the toasted bread before the cheese mixture.

SERVES 4

Melt half the butter in a pan and fry the leeks till they're soft. They can be just beginning to colour but don't let them burn, as they will taste bitter.

Melt in the rest of the butter and stir in the flour. Stirring constantly with a wooden spoon, gradually add the beer and the milk to make a basic sauce. Bring to a gentle simmer and stir in the mustard and cheese. Keep stirring until you have a smooth thick sauce. Grind in a good amount of fresh black pepper and turn off the heat to let it all sit while you prepare the other ingredients.

Lightly toast the bread, spread each slice with the cheese mixture and slide under a hot grill until the topping is golden and bubbling.

Meanwhile, assuming there is more than one cook in the kitchen, somebody else should be either frying or poaching the eggs, ready to put them on top as the slices emerge from the grill. Finish with a good grind of fresh black pepper and a shake of Tabasco.

50g butter
1 leek, washed and diced in 1cm pieces
1 tbsp flour
75ml beer
75ml milk
1 tsp English mustard powder
150g Cheddar cheese, grated
8 slices of good bread
4 eggs
Tabasco sauce, to serve

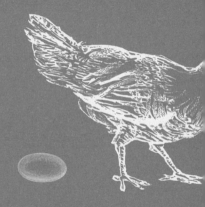

Parsnips

Sweet and soothing autumn warmers

Thank heavens for the distinctive honeyed taste of parsnips, which keeps us going through the autumn and on in to the winter months. Parsnips like to be roasted or mashed, come in to their own in a curry, bring texture and flavour to stews and soups, and also, surprisingly, work very well in salads (see recipe on page 203).

Comfort foods come in many packages and although most of them are at the soft and yielding end of the spectrum — such as anything topped with mashed potato or accompanied by custard — I would say that a dish of sticky, slender, caramelized, slightly blackened parsnips should also be included.

As should a mildly curried and creamy parsnip soup. And, as if by magic, here is just the recipe — parsnip and apples — heaven and earth.

Indian spiced parsnip and apple soup

Sweet, warming and easy to prepare, this is a good midweek soup. Anyone working at home, sitting for hours at a computer – this one's for you.

SERVES 4

Preheat the oven to 180°C/160°C fan/gas mark 4.

Toss the apple pieces in the sunflower oil, place in a baking tray and roast for 20 minutes or until they are soft, stirring them around halfway through the cooking time to ensure they brown evenly.

Meanwhile, heat the olive oil in a large pan, add the diced vegetables and cook gently with the lid on for about 20 minutes. Stir in the curry powder and cook for a further 3 minutes, then pour in the stock. Bring to the boil and add the roasted apples and honey. Simmer for 5 minutes, then allow to cool slightly before liquidizing. Return to the pan to reheat and season to taste.

Serve with some good crusty bread and a swirl of cream, if you're feeling decadent.

3 medium cooking apples
   (approx. 500g), peeled, cored
   and cut in chunks
I tsp sunflower oil
2 tbsp olive oil
2 onions, diced
I stick of celery, diced
2 potatoes, peeled and cut
   in small chunks
3 large parsnips, peeled
   and diced
2 tsp curry powder
I.5 litres vegetable stock
I tbsp honey
single cream, to serve (optional)

Pumpkins and squash
Taxi to Prince Charming's?

Formerly used for dropping girls off at castles or for being spooky at Halloween, over the last few years pumpkins have found their rightful place in the kitchen, where they belong, bringing colour and texture to all sorts of recipes. What took them so long? Sweet, colourful and nutritious, they are perfect for autumn days.

There's something magical about them too: from one small seed you get an extraordinary plant that spreads in no time, with enormous umbrella-like leaves, curling tendrils and then, finally, little green or yellow globes that grow and grow, sometimes so much that we can barely lift them. But lift them we do, because from that one strange and fantastical orb comes a huge array of delicious dishes.

Pumpkins and all their sisterly varieties of squash should pretty much always start off in the oven. If you're using them for soup, you can hack them in to large chunks, scoop away the seeds and roast them, skins on, with a drizzle of olive oil or ground nut oil for 45 minutes or so in a fairly hot oven (200°C/180°C fan/gas mark 6) until tender. Then, when they're cooked, it's easy to peel away the skin. For adding to pizzas, curries and tarts or stuffing in to pies, you're best peeling and cubing them first.

Cut in crescent moons and roasted with a sprinkle of cinnamon and olive oil, they're good eaten just as they are. But they also go brilliantly with other vegetables and masses of different flavours and textures: think chorizo, butter beans, rice, nuts, eggs, goat's cheese — indeed any cheese, especially blue. They have a particular affinity with Asian flavours, which is why Thai butternut squash soup and butternut squash and coconut curry (see recipes on pages 293 and 246) are the stuff of culinary dreams.

To roast fresh chestnuts, start by buying slightly more than the recipe requires. Make slits in each chestnut with a sharp knife and roast them in a hot oven (200°C/180°C fan/gas mark 6) for about 25 minutes. When they are cool enough to handle, peel the outer and inner layers off.

Pumpkin, chestnut and cranberry risotto

Pumpkins and squash like nothing better than a creamy rice dish to which they can add colour, texture and flavour.

So much has been written about the right way to make risotto that people could be forgiven for thinking it's too much effort. But I would say that there are just two essentials. First, you must use proper risotto rice, because you need its high starch content to get that unctuous creaminess. Second, you will need to stir for at least 20, maybe 30 minutes, because the secret to a subtle, soothing risotto of melting smoothness is in the stirring — with a glass of wine to hand, somebody to chat to nearby and the knowledge that there's a delicious supper heading your way soon.

SERVES 6

Preheat the oven to 180°C/160°C fan/gas mark 4.

Place the pumpkin, rosemary and thyme on a baking tray, add a good slug or two of olive oil and mix with your hands to ensure that everything is well coated in oil to stop it burning. Roast for 45 minutes or so until tender. Allow to cool for 10 minutes, then remove the skin and cut the pumpkin in 1cm cubes.

In a large, heavy-based saucepan, gently fry the shallot and garlic in olive oil without colouring them. Turn the heat up, add the rice and stir until it looks glossy, about 3 minutes. Turn the heat down again and add the white wine. Continue to stir until the wine is absorbed and then add the hot stock, a ladleful at a time, stirring constantly. Wait until each ladleful has been absorbed by the rice before adding the next — it's a slow process, so you'll probably be adding stock and stirring for about 20-30 minutes in total.

When you have about 500ml of stock left, gently stir in the roasted pumpkin cubes and continue to add the stock ladle by ladle, stirring all the time. Before adding the last ladleful of stock, taste the rice to ensure it is cooked through (it should be tender with just a little 'bite' in the middle). Stir in the chestnuts, cranberries and the last of the stock. Finally, once the chestnuts and cranberries are heated through and the last of the stock has been absorbed, add the mascarpone and 100g of the Parmesan and stir through. Serve immediately with the remaining Parmesan and some freshly ground black pepper sprinkled across the top.

1.2kg pumpkin, quartered and sliced with skin on
2 sprigs of fresh rosemary
3 sprigs of fresh thyme
2-3 tbsp olive oil, plus more for roasting
1 shallot, diced
1 garlic clove, finely chopped
300g Arborio rice
100ml white wine
1.25 litres hot vegetable stock
200g vacuum-packed or fresh roasted chestnuts, broken in pieces
75g fresh, frozen or dried cranberries, roughly chopped
150g mascarpone cheese
150g Parmesan, grated

Figs
Star quality

Glamorous and sexy, figs are the Sophia Lorens of the food world. And, like Sophia, they're star material. Best eaten just as they are, perfectly ripe, or with other equally classy Tuscan hills-type numbers such as walnuts, honey and ricotta, they are complete show-stealers.

They're expensive (unless you happen to have a tree that produces edible figs, and some lucky people do) and are in season only briefly, both of which only add to their celebrity status. We just have to be grateful they don't insist on 24-hour security and a larger trailer.

And there's more: figs won't ripen once they're picked, so they have to be transported — carefully — when they're at their best and you can imagine how little they like that. Easier to move to a country where they can grow and ripen in the sun and where we can just pluck them from the tree.

Fig and mascarpone bundles

Figs and mascarpone cheese with basil, wrapped in golden puff pastry, plus pine nuts and Parma ham: every inch an Italian beauty.

MAKES 6

Preheat the oven to 190°C/170°C fan/gas mark 5.

First snip off the top of the figs and discard the stalks. Sit them upright and slice downwards twice, almost to the bottom, to make a cross. Toast the pine nuts by dry-frying them briefly until they are golden – this will only take a few minutes. Set them aside.

Roll out the pastry to a rectangle 26 x 39cm and cut it in 6 squares each measuring 13 x 13cm. If you've bought pre-rolled pastry, you may need to roll it a little further to bring it up to size. Brush each square with some of the egg wash.

Build the bundles by placing half a teaspoonful of pesto and then a spoonful of mascarpone in the middle of each pastry square. Add a couple of basil leaves. Sit a fig on top and scatter with a few pine nuts. Lay a slice of ham over the fig and spread another half teaspoonful of pesto across the top. Bring the four corners of pastry up and over the contents and squeeze together along the seams to seal. Brush each bundle with more egg wash.

Place the bundles on a baking tray and bake for 40-45 minutes, or until they are golden. They're best eaten warm and served with a dainty salad.

6 large figs
25g pine nuts, toasted
375g ready-made puff pastry
1 egg, beaten and mixed
 with 1 tbsp milk
6 tsp pesto
150g mascarpone cheese
a handful of basil leaves
6 slices of Parma ham

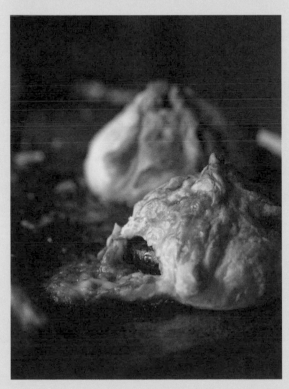

Apples

Fruity little numbers

Apples are one of the glories of an English autumn, not only to look at – on trees, stacked in wooden crates outside our stores, in pies – but also for their all-round grab-and-go appeal. Apple trees love our climate and so, pretty much whatever is thrown at them, they'll deliver crunchy, juicy, packed with flavour fruit.

Times and tastes have changed and a lot of the older varieties have fallen out of fashion, which is a shame. Beauty of Bath, Egremont Russet, Worcester Pearmain – bring them back for their names alone! Happily, apple growers are pushing and producing to get more English varieties back in the shops.

There are seasons within seasons for apples, so as one variety peaks, another is getting ready to take centre stage. Between them they keep the show going for many months: Discovery, Cox's, Russets, Braeburn, Bramleys – one way and another, there's an excuse to get some sort of apple-based pudding on the table night after night for the foreseeable future.

As luck would have it, apples are more than willing to jump in to bed with all sorts. Taking advantage of their slender grasp on fidelity, we can mix things up with a wide array of flavours and textures. Cinnamon, crispy buttery toppings and vanilla ice cream all bring out the best in an apple, as do muesli, currants, dates, warming spices, fresh or crystallized ginger, vanilla, brown sugar, honey, golden syrup and cream. Apples like to be fried in butter, roasted alongside pork, wrapped in pastry, covered in breadcrumbs, packed in to crumbles and eaten, just as they are, while you wait for your train at the station. They're that tarty.

An apple a day

A crisp apple and a hunk of cheese. These two really do have something going on. To my mind, nothing sums up autumn in England more than a polished Russet, eaten with a piece of blue cheese, a handful of walnuts and a glass of port. Thanks very much, don't mind if I do.

Sliced and fried in butter, apples can be spooned on to toasted brioche or in to pancakes (see page 210). They can also be topped with creamy yoghurt and a sprinkle of cinnamon and sugar.

Finely grated apple, skin and all, is good stirred in to granola and yoghurt for breakfast.

Windfalls are perfect for juicing to drink now, freeze for later or turn in to healthy juice lollies.

Apples and blackberries love each other. See page 196 for how to make a quick blackberry purée and also a blackberry and roasted apple juice.

Apple and potato rösti

You can top these golden discs with all sorts — a poached egg being at the top of my list. Crispy purple sprouting broccoli stems (see recipe on page 237) are great with rösti, covered with plenty of Parmesan or strong Cheddar cheese. Also try any of the following: wilted spinach, pancetta, flaked smoked mackerel, roasted root vegetables with crumbled blue cheese or feta and pine nuts. Make a fresh salad to go with them and you have a wholesome and inexpensive supper.

MAKES 6-8

Coarsely grate the potatoes — King Edward's or Maris Piper are good. Rinse well, then dry well by squeezing between your hands to extract the moisture, and put in a bowl. Peel and grate the apple, add to the potato and season well. Stir in the flour, egg and chives.

With floury hands, divide the mixture in to 6-8 balls and then flatten them in to circles, each roughly 10cm in diameter.

3 medium-large floury
   potatoes (approx. 500g),
   peeled
1 large crisp apple
4 tbsp plain flour
1 large egg, beaten
2 tbsp chives, snipped (optional)
6 tbsp vegetable oil

Heat the oil in a frying pan and fry the rösti for 3-4 minutes on each side until golden. They are best served straight from the pan while still sizzling hot. If you're not going to dish up straight away, you can transfer the cooked rösti from the pan to a baking tray in the oven on a low heat to keep warm until you're ready to roll.

Alternatively, if you want to prepare these in advance, fry them lightly (a couple of minutes each side should do) before cooling and chilling in the fridge. You can then ovenbake them at 190°C/170°C fan/gas mark 5 for 12-14 minutes, until golden, crispy and piping hot.

Apples baked with fruit and nuts

Baked apples can go in the oven along with a roast or whatever else is in there, so long as the temperature is around the middling mark. They're equally good whether you eat them hot as pudding with vanilla ice cream, or cold from the fridge for a fruity breakfast the next day. And of course there's nothing to stop you having them with vanilla ice cream for breakfast, if you're in the mood for living dangerously.

SERVES 6

Soak the fruit — this can be a haphazard mix of whatever you have around: dates, prunes, apricots, raisins, sultanas, cranberries — in the port or apple juice for several hours, preferably overnight.

Preheat the oven to 180°C/160°C fan/gas mark 4.

Line a deep baking tin with enough foil to come up and over the apples once they are in. Wash and core the apples, score a line horizontally around their middles to stop them exploding while they're cooking, and place them in the baking tin. Drain the soaked fruit, reserving the port or apple juice.

6 heaped tbsp chopped dried fruit

150ml port or apple juice

6 large Bramley apples (approx. 220g each)

2 tbsp chopped nuts and seeds

2 tbsp honey or golden syrup

Add nuts and seeds — try slivered hazelnuts or almonds with pumpkin and sunflower seeds — to the soaked fruit and pack the mixture in to the hollow centre of the apples. Don't worry if it overflows. Drizzle each apple with honey or golden syrup and spoon the reserved port or apple juice across the top.

Loosely fold the foil over the apples and bake for 40 minutes. Open the foil and bake uncovered for a further 10 minutes, until the apples are cooked but not collapsing. Allow the dish to sit for 10 minutes before serving with a generous topping of vanilla ice cream.

Apples and caramel

Yet another of those horse and carriage combinations: a stack of crunchy, just-sliced apples alongside a bowl of home-made caramel sauce. This is one of those rare child-friendly puddings that actually has a healthy element — in that they're dipping fresh fruit in the caramel as opposed to, say, chocolate fingers. Cox's or Crispins, apples with a slightly tart flavour, are a good foil for the sweet caramel sauce.

This sauce is also wonderful with pancakes and waffles, or for something even more decadent, it is great with vanilla ice cream or panacotta.

SERVES 4

Put the butter and sugar in a pan over a low heat. Stir until they are completely melted together. Continue stirring while you add the cream. Allow the sauce to cool a little and then pour in to a shallow dish.

While the sauce is cooling, core and slice the apples and serve alongside the caramel sauce.

25g butter
100g brown sugar
75ml single cream
4 eating apples (or more)

Windfall chutney

A very good and flavoursome chutney for the fruit that didn't make it to the table.

MAKES 4-6 JARS

Core the fruit and chop in to bite-sized pieces. There's no need to peel it, but dispose of any tough or bruised skin. Cover with a good drizzle of lemon juice to prevent the pieces from browning, then set them aside.

Put all the other ingredients apart from the pine nuts and mustard seeds in to a heavy-based pan. Add a few twists of black pepper and bring slowly to the boil, being careful not to let the sugar catch and burn on the bottom of the pan. Simmer gently, stirring regularly with a wooden spoon. After about 20 minutes the mixture should have thickened and you will be able to see the bottom of the pan when you draw the wooden spoon through.

Toast the pine nuts by dry-frying for a couple of minutes till they're golden, and then add them to the chutney, along with the chopped fruit and mustard seeds. Cook for a further 30 minutes or so, until the chutney has reached a good medium to thick consistency.

Let the chutney cool slightly before pouring in to sterilized jars and sealing with plastic-coated screw-on lids (the vinegar will spoil metal jam pot lids). Ideally, it should be stored in a dark cupboard for about 3 months, but can be eaten sooner, depending on your preference and on how long you can wait.

●●●●●●●●●●●●●●●●●●●●●●●●●●●●●●●

To sterilize jars, wash them in hot soapy water, rinse and shake off the excess water. Put them on a baking tray in a low oven for 10 minutes. Alternatively, you can run them through a hot wash in a dishwasher.

●●●●●●●●●●●●●●●●●●●●●●●●●●●●●●●

10-12 apples or a mixture
  of apples and pears
  (approx. 1.2kg)
the zest of 2 lemons,
  plus juice for drizzling
the zest of 2 oranges
550ml cider vinegar
400g soft brown sugar
4 large red onions, diced
4 star anise
4 bay leaves
4 thumbs of fresh ginger,
  peeled and finely chopped
2 tsp 5-spice powder
200g pine nuts, toasted
2 tsp black mustard seeds

Bill's autumn champion

Pears

Conference call

The reason pears are sometimes seen as poor relations to apples is that they are quite high maintenance. They need to be picked before they ripen and then, when they are ripe, they are very touchy and bruise easily, making transportation that bit more complicated.

If you're hoping to eat a pear just as it is, the trick is to catch it at the right moment. They sit there hard and unyielding for ages, and then the next time you check, they've gone beyond and are good for blending in to a smoothie and not much else. But a pear of perfect ripeness, cut through with a sharp knife and eaten delicate slice by delicate slice, is a gift.

But when you're not hungry for a perfect pear moment, you don't need to worry too much about their erratic ripening process, because there's a whole world of dishes to play with once you start cooking, and they make soothing puddings for autumn and beyond.

A perfect pear

Raw or roasted, pears are good with big-flavoured cheeses such as Stilton, feta and goat's cheese, with nuts – especially walnuts and hazelnuts, and in salads, bringing contrast and a gentle sweetness.

Poached pears – very 1970s – make a classy-looking pudding and are really easy. Poach them in red wine with some cinnamon and vanilla or in a simple sugar syrup, and then coat in a rich, shiny chocolate sauce. What a pudding.

Peeled and sliced, pears love being covered in cream and brown sugar and blasted under the grill, and when cooked in the oven in a custard, tart or sponge, their consistency becomes almost fudge-like.

And, to prove the point, on the next page, there's a recipe for a pear custard tart.

Pear custard tart with toasted cinnamon walnuts

Pears work really well in a tart, their delicate flavour sitting very happily in a creamy custard. You don't have to add the cinnamon walnuts, but they do bring even more of autumn to this lovely pudding.

SERVES 6

To make the pastry, rub the flour and butter together in a mixing bowl or whizz them together in a food processor. Stir in the icing sugar and lemon zest. Add the egg yolks and mix to form a dough. If it's too dry, add a splash of water. Knead briefly until smooth, wrap in cling film and chill in the fridge for 30 minutes.

Preheat the oven to 180°C/160°C fan/gas mark 4 and leave a baking sheet in there to get hot.

Roll out the pastry and use to line a 25cm flan tin, pricking the pastry a few times with a fork. Place a sheet of baking parchment over the pastry, pour in some baking beans and bake blind for 10-15 minutes. Remove the beans and baking parchment and return the pastry to the oven for 5 minutes. Remove and leave to cool for 20 minutes.

Peel, core and slice the pears and arrange the slices in the pastry case. Whisk the eggs in a large bowl, add the cream and whisk again. Add the sugar and cinnamon, mix thoroughly and pour this custard over the pears. Finish with a light dusting of nutmeg.

Place the tin on a baking sheet and slide carefully in to the oven. Bake for 10 minutes, then turn the oven down to 150°C/130°C fan/gas mark 2 and bake for a further 20 minutes, until the custard is just set.

Combine the sugar and cinnamon in a bowl. Slowly toast the walnut pieces in a frying pan until they start to brown. Remove from the pan and allow them to cool, then toss them in the sugar and cinnamon mix.

Sprinkle the cinnamon walnuts across the top of the finished tart and serve with a jug of single cream or crème fraîche alongside.

* To use up the leftover egg whites, you could make meringues (see recipe on page 28) or lemon meringue roulade (see recipe on page 70). If this is pudding overload, you could mix the whites with some whole eggs for omelettes or scrambling. Covered egg whites will keep in the fridge for 3-4 days, or you can freeze them for up to 6 months (defrost them slowly in the fridge before you use them).

FOR THE PASTRY
200g plain flour, sifted
100g unsalted butter, chilled and cubed
2 tbsp icing sugar
the zest of half a lemon
2 large egg yolks, beaten*

FOR THE FILLING
3 medium pears
2 large eggs
300ml whipping cream
125g caster sugar
1 tsp cinnamon
a dusting of nutmeg

FOR THE TOPPING
1 dsp caster sugar
1 tsp cinnamon
100g walnuts, chopped in smallish pieces

Blackberries

Something for nothing

Long before the days of the BlackBerry, there were blackberries and blackberrying — coming home with purple-stained fingers, arms and legs covered in scratches. Of course, blackberries are still there for the picking, and it's as enjoyable a way as any of spending an hour or two on one of those weirdly hot, post-summer-tipping-in-to-autumn days you can get in September. You just need to know where there's a decent crop and off you go with a few plastic tubs. Good food for nothing!

What you will come home with is a motley selection of berries — some small and pretty tasteless, some sharp, others plump and glossy and packed with fruitiness. None of them will look like the cultivated whoppers in the supermarket, but they're all good for whatever you have in mind on the eating front.

Blackberry ways

Soak hedgerow blackberries in water with a liberal sprinkling of salt for several hours to remove any bugs. Then rinse them thoroughly, remove any stalks and put them in a saucepan with a good splash of water and some sugar – the amounts will depend on how many you are cooking and how sweet you like them. Simmer slowly with the lid on to break the berries down. When they're cooked, allow them to cool slightly and then squish them through a sieve to remove the seeds.

If you've picked more blackberries than you know what to do with, you can always make jam. Or you can purée and freeze them to use for puddings right through the autumn.

Simple and soothing, a bowl of creamy Greek yoghurt with some warm blackberry purée spooned across the top and a sprinkle of golden caster sugar to finish is in the realms of ambrosia.

Traditionally, blackberries are paired with apples, which soften the flavour and also help the berries to go further. So, if your pickings are scant rather than rich, you can purée some apples along with the blackberries for pies and crumbles, or to use as a topping for porridge.

Blackberry and roasted apple juice

SERVES 2

Preheat the oven to 180°C/160°C fan/gas mark 4.

Peel and core the apples – Cox's are good – then cut them in chunks. Tip in to a bowl, drizzle over a tablespoonful of honey and the vanilla extract and stir well to coat.

Scatter the apple chunks in a baking tray and roast for 25 minutes, stirring once or twice to make sure they are evenly browned, then remove the tray from the oven. When they are cool, place in a blender with the blackberries and the apple juice. Blend and taste for sweetness, adding brown sugar or extra honey if you think it's needed.

For a smoother juice, pass the mixture through a sieve. If you feel it's too thick, add more apple juice and stir through or blitz to combine.

3 medium eating apples
  (approx. 300g)
1 tbsp runny honey,
  plus extra to taste
½ tsp vanilla extract
250g blackberries, rinsed
  and tidied
100ml apple juice
brown sugar, to taste

Goldilocks – a girl with good taste

Breakfast

For stoking your fires and keeping you going until lunchtime, for health-giving benefits and simple, minimal-ingredient cooking, porridge wins on every count as the perfect breakfast, especially as the weather starts to turn and colder mornings creep up on us.

Devotees each have their own method of cooking, their own strong ideas about the extras. And they may look at you with contempt if you disagree. Puritans say you add nothing, sensualists add dried figs and berries, toasted nuts, maple syrup, double cream, brown sugar – maybe not all at the same time as that would be delicious, but eccentric.

Remember tins of Ideal or Carnation evaporated milk? And the triangular holes we made in the top for pouring? Suffice to say, that was what I poured all over my porridge when I was growing up and none the wiser.

Bill's porridge

Play around with the quantities here to get your porridge just right (as Goldilocks would say). Adding the instant porridge will give a really creamy texture.

SERVES 1

Pour the milk in a heavy-based pan and add the oats and salt. Simmer over a low heat for about 5 minutes, stirring with a wooden spoon, until the oats are cooked through and the porridge is smooth. Add the instant porridge and some more milk (or water) if the mixture is too thick, and allow to cook for another couple of minutes. You may want to add more milk or water at this stage, depending on how you like your porridge.

300ml milk (or milk and water), plus more to taste
50g porridge oats
a pinch of salt
1 tbsp instant porridge (Ready Brek or similar)

Serve with a generous helping of stewed fruit (see recipe opposite) and a drizzle or sprinkle of golden syrup, honey, brown sugar, maple syrup or pomegranate molasses.

Stewed fruit

You could, in theory, have a jar of stewed fruit in the fridge, on standby, throughout the year. Not just for topping porridge, but for instant puddings, to go with yoghurt or for snacking.

This is an autumnal version featuring a mix of fresh and dried fruit. But it could be apples, sugar and cinnamon, or just apples and pears. A winter mix would feature more dried fruit, perhaps with some fresh apples (or not), and in midsummer you could take advantage of the ripe stone fruit and make up a jar of poached nectarines and/or peaches with vanilla.

MAKES 1 LARGE KILNER JAR (8–10 PORTIONS)

500g mixed fresh and dried fruit, such
  as apples, blackberries and pears
  with dried figs, apricots and prunes
1 cinnamon stick
3 cloves

1 star anise
2 handfuls of fresh or
  frozen cranberries (optional)
1 cup of apple juice
the zest and juice of 1 large orange

Mix everything together in a bowl and let it stand for a couple of hours if you have time. Otherwise, skip straight to the chase and put all the ingredients in a saucepan and simmer gently for a good 30 minutes. Leave to cool and steep before transferring to a Kilner jar, tupperware container or similar to store in the fridge, where it should keep for a good week or so.

Autumn salads

Autumn produce is perfect for creating colourful salads that are full of flavour, mixing fruit and vegetables, both fresh and cooked.

And, as with all seasons, it's a tale of two halves, with early autumn ingredients such as figs and even tomatoes giving way to more robust produce like pumpkins, mushrooms and root vegetables. The days are getting shorter but the kitchen can still provide a whoop of vitality: add new-season walnuts, seeds, raisins and dried cranberries for variety, citrus juice for zing and herbs for contrast.

 ### Wouldn't it be grate

Through the autumn and on in to the winter, keep your grater to hand for making quick, fresh salads. Coleslaws are good all year round, but definitely come in to their own during the colder months. Let your larder be your guide when it comes to slaws: cabbages are the mainstay and then it's whatever you have to hand or fancy – carrot, beetroot, apple, pear, dried fruit, nuts, seeds – mixed well together and all lightly stirred through with a citrus or yoghurt-based dressing. Here are a couple of very simple ideas:

Grate equal quantities of carrot and Cheddar cheese, combine well in a salad dish and, just before serving, sprinkle a spoonful of sesame seeds across the top. Children love this salad and it's very good as a topping for baked potatoes.

Grate some celeriac and immediately toss it in lemon juice to keep it from browning while you grate an equal quantity of raw beetroot. Sit the grated beetroot on top of the celeriac and drizzle with some olive oil and lemon juice.

Spiced cauliflower and chickpea salad

SERVES 4-6

Cook the cauliflower florets with the turmeric in simmering
water for about 8-10 minutes — it should still retain some bite.
In the meantime, cook the cavolo nero in simmering water
in a separate pan for about 6 minutes. Drain both and allow
to cool.

Heat the oil in a frying pan and add the cumin seeds. Cook
for 30 seconds, turning with a wooden spoon, then add the
harissa — Rose harissa is good — and the saffron (if using).
Cook for a further minute, stirring continuously.

Combine the cooled cauliflower, cavolo nero, chickpeas,
coriander, sunblush tomatoes, lemon juice and zest in a
bowl, then stir in the cumin and harissa mixture. Tip in
to a serving dish and garnish by arranging the preserved
lemon slices on top.

1 medium cauliflower,
  cut in florets
a pinch of turmeric
400g cavolo nero, cut in
  2cm lengths
1 tsp vegetable oil
1 tsp cumin seeds
100g harissa paste
1 tsp saffron (optional)
1 x 400g tin of chickpeas,
  drained
a good handful of fresh
  coriander, roughly chopped
150g sunblush tomatoes,
  roughly chopped
the juice and zest of 3 lemons
half a preserved lemon,
  finely sliced

Honey-roast pear and parsnip salad

This sweet and savoury salad is perfect just as it is or served with roast pork or gammon. It also works well as an accompaniment to hot or cold roast chicken.

SERVES 4

Preheat the oven to 180°C/160°C fan/gas mark 4.

Toss the parsnips in half the honey or maple syrup and put them on a baking tray to roast in the oven for about 15 minutes. Toss the pears in the rest of the honey or syrup and add them to the parsnips to cook together for a further 10 minutes. Remove the tray from the oven and leave the pears and parsnips to cool slightly.

Put the radicchio in an ovenproof dish and layer the still-warm pears and parsnips on top. Sprinkle with the crumbled cheese, then whack the dish under a very hot grill for a minute, just to get the cheese melting. Remove from the grill and scatter the rocket leaves across the top.

Whisk the dressing ingredients together and spoon over the salad.

2 medium parsnips, peeled and cut in strips
1 tbsp honey or maple syrup
2 pears, peeled, cored and quartered
a small head of radicchio, torn apart
100g Stilton or another blue cheese, crumbled
a handful of rocket leaves

FOR THE DRESSING
1 tsp white wine vinegar
1 tsp Dijon mustard
1 tsp honey
2 tsp olive oil
2 tsp lemon or lime juice

Warm pumpkin and lentil salad with goat's cheese

SERVES 4

Preheat the oven to 180°C/160°C fan/gas mark 4.

Put the lentils in a small pan with 500ml of water. Bring to the boil, cover and simmer for 30 minutes until they are tender.

Meanwhile, put the pumpkin chunks in a baking tray with the onion quarters, drizzle with two tablespoons of olive oil, sprinkle with the cinnamon and season with sea salt and freshly ground black pepper. Mix with your hands to make sure everything is well coated in the oil. Bake for 15-20 minutes or so until the pumpkin is tender and the onion is beginning to blacken.

When the lentils are cooked, drain them and stir in the remaining tablespoonful of olive oil, the mustard, vinegar and parsley.

Arrange the rocket leaves on a serving plate. Spread the pumpkin and onion mixture across the rocket, spoon over the lentils and, finally, crumble the goat's cheese across the top.

120g Puy lentils
1 small pumpkin (approx. 800g), peeled, deseeded and cut in bite-sized chunks
2 large red onions, quartered
3 tbsp olive oil
1 tsp cinnamon
1 tsp wholegrain mustard
1 tbsp balsamic vinegar
a handful of flat-leaf parsley, roughly chopped
50g wild rocket
200g goat's cheese

'I'm starving!'

Tea after school

Oh, the sad inevitability that is going back to school after the summer holidays, when grubby T-shirts and flip-flops are replaced by crisp new uniforms and shoes, late-to-bedtimes are ousted by routine, and lolling around doing nothing is swapped for homework. Children spend the summer term counting the days and weeks till the summer holidays and yet, as the summer days creep towards September, they're excited about going back to school, torn between the two.

Once they're back – grumbling about new teachers (really, she is the worst person *ever*), making new friends, getting to grips with new timetables – two things are certain: they're tired and they're always ravenous when they get home. What's required is quick and easy face-filling food.

Fish finger sandwiches

Fish finger sandwiches were on our first ever menu at Bill's and they're still there because they are one of the most popular dishes we sell. When you're hungry, they just do the job. Here's our recipe.

MAKES 4

12 good-quality frozen fish fingers
8 slices of thick white farmhouse bread
4 tbsp tartare sauce
half a crisp lettuce, shredded
4 tbsp tomato ketchup
1 lemon, halved

Preheat the grill and grill the fish fingers for 3-4 minutes each side.
When they're nearly done, toast the bread.

Spread four slices of toast with the tartare sauce. Top each slice with
some shredded lettuce, three fish fingers, a tablespoonful of ketchup and a squeeze
of fresh lemon juice. Finish off with the remaining slices of toast. A real belter
of a sandwich.

Treacle tart with apple and vanilla

Coming home from school, a big slice of home-made treacle tart is always going to hit the spot. Or you can save it for after supper. For tea, it's best served warm just as it is. As a pudding, it's good hot or warm with custard, cream or vanilla ice cream.

SERVES 6-8

Preheat the oven to 180°C/160°C fan/gas mark 4 and leave a baking sheet in the oven to get hot.

Start by rubbing the flour and butter together in a large bowl or whizzing them in a food processor until the mixture resembles breadcrumbs. Then stir in the icing sugar and lemon zest. Add the egg yolks and mix until you have a dough. If it's too dry, add a splash of water. Knead briefly until smooth, wrap in cling film and chill in the fridge for 30 minutes.

While the dough is chilling, place the golden syrup, the cream and the lemon zest and juice in a saucepan over a low heat and simmer gently for 5 minutes. Remove the pan from the heat, add the breadcrumbs, grated apple and vanilla extract, give things a good stir, then leave to stand for 10 minutes.

Roll out the pastry on a lightly floured surface and use to line a 25cm diameter flan tin, pricking the pastry base a few times with a fork. Place a sheet of baking parchment over the pastry and cover with baking beans. Bake blind for 10-15 minutes, remove the paper and beans and return the flan tin to the oven for 5 more minutes.

Remove the pastry case from the oven, pour the treacle mix in to it and bake for 30 minutes or until golden brown.

* To use up the leftover egg whites, you could make meringues (see recipe on page 28) or lemon meringue roulade (see page 70). However, this might be pudding overload, so instead you could mix the whites with some whole eggs for omelettes or scrambling. Covered egg whites will keep in the fridge for 3-4 days, or you can freeze them for up to 6 months (defrost them slowly in the fridge before you use them).

FOR THE PASTRY
200g plain flour, sifted
100g unsalted butter, chilled and cubed
2 tbsp icing sugar
the zest of 1 lemon
2 large eggs yolks*, beaten

FOR THE FILLING
450g golden syrup
170ml single cream
the zest and juice of 1 lemon
50g breadcrumbs
250g apples, grated
1 tsp vanilla extract

Pancakes

I sometimes think we don't pay enough attention to pancakes, especially given that they are very cheap to make from store cupboard ingredients, can be used to form a base for, or wrap around, a huge number of ingredients, swing either way in the sweet and savoury stakes and can be prepared in advance. I mean, come on.

And, if you're up for the challenge, they're also very good after school, particularly when you involve the children in flipping and filling. If there are friends round for tea, even better. Just prepare — in advance — more batter than you could ever have thought they would get through and you're away. Or rather, you'll wish you were away.

To avoid standing over the frying pan, cooking as fast as the pancakes are being eaten at the table and with everything getting a bit tense, you can prepare in advance — either really in advance and stacking them in the fridge, loosely wrapped in foil (for up to 24 hours), or somewhat in advance, to keep warm in the oven. Whichever, making the batter ahead and allowing it to stand for at least 30 minutes is definitely a good idea, as it really does make a difference to the lightness.

Oh the glory that is a bit o' batter. Because that's only the beginning. You can go down the fajitas route, you can make lace-like French-style crêpes or little Asian pancakes for dipping or Peking duck. And all that before we've even started on sweet pancakes: from Welsh cakes to paratha, every culture does something that involves flipping some simple ingredients in a frying pan.

Then of course there's the question of what you put on your pancakes. Start with some tasty savoury fillings then move on to sweet toppings, and hey presto, you've got your entire meal wrapped up.

Leek and bacon buckwheat pancakes

To start the pancake ball rolling, here's a hearty dish featuring a buckwheat batter.
I like using buckwheat — its nutty flavour is very good in savoury pancakes and also, with quite
a rich filling, it's nice to balance things out with something a little bit healthy and wholesome.

If you feel like it, you can top each sauce-covered pancake with a fried egg for a final flourish.

MAKES 6

Sift the flours in to a large bowl, add the salt and make a well
in the middle. Beat the egg and milk together in a jug. Slowly
pour this mixture in to the well, whisking as you go. Stir in
the melted butter, cover and let the batter rest in the
fridge for 30 minutes.

Heat a small amount of oil in a large frying pan. When the
pan is hot, add half a ladle of the batter and swirl it around
so it covers the bottom of the pan. This may be a tougher
job than usual, as the batter will be a bit thicker than for
ordinary pancakes. When the underneath has turned golden
brown, flip the pancake over with the aid of a palette knife
to cook the other side.

Add a little more oil to the pan for each pancake, stacking
the cooked pancakes on a plate in a low temperature oven to
keep warm until you are ready to fill them.

Once you've made the pancakes, melt the butter in a pan
and gently cook the leeks for about 10 minutes, until they
are soft. Try to avoid letting them colour or stick to the pan,
adding a little water if they do start to stick. Add the cream
and season. Stir everything together gently and remove from
the heat. Stir in the cheese and set aside.

In another pan, sauté the lardons in their own fat until golden.
Add to the leek mixture and gently warm on a low heat.

To serve, place each pancake on a plate and top with some of
the bacon and leek mixture, folding the edges of the pancake
over or leaving it open, as you prefer.

FOR THE PANCAKES
60g plain flour
50g buckwheat flour
½ tsp salt
1 medium egg
300ml milk
15g butter, melted
sunflower oil, for frying

FOR THE FILLING
a generous knob of butter
2 large leeks, washed
  and sliced
6 tbsp double cream
100g Gruyère or
  Comté cheese
100g smoked bacon lardons

Pancake possibilities

First up on the savoury pancake front has to be tomato sauce (see recipe on page 85): pancakes filled with just about anything, from fish to chicken, bolognese and roasted vegetables, smothered with a tomato sauce, sprinkled with lots of grated Cheddar and then flashed under the grill.

Next in line is a rich cheese sauce. Filled pancakes sardined into a dish and covered with a flavourful cheese sauce is a very good autumn supper. Generally, cheese and pancakes are a happy pair – mozzarella, strong Cheddar, crumbled feta, blue cheese.

As for fillings, plenty of vegetables lend themselves to the pancake experience, but the better bedfellows are leeks, mushrooms, squash, peppers, spinach, broccoli, purple sprouting broccoli and peas. The same goes for herbs, especially parsley, basil, coriander and dill.

And three more for good luck:

Grilled salmon, cream cheese and dill.

Wilted spinach and ricotta.

Garlic mushrooms.

Flipping fantastic

For sweet pancakes, you can keep it simple and traditional with caster sugar and lemon juice, or you can go fancy by stirring berries through the batter – blueberries work well, as they hold their shape – and getting creative with the fillings.

Here's a light and easy pancake recipe, just what you need as the base for any number of sweet fillings.

MAKES 8

Sift the flour in to a large bowl, stir in a pinch of salt, make a well in the centre and break the egg in to the well. Add some of the milk and gradually stir the liquids in to the flour using a wooden spoon until you have a smooth thick batter. Beat this well, then add the rest of the milk, beating as you go until you have a smooth gloopy batter. Pour it in a jug, cover and let it rest in the fridge for 30 minutes if there's time.

125g plain flour
a pinch of salt
I large egg
300ml milk
sunflower oil,
  for frying

Heat a small amount of oil in a large frying pan. When the pan is hot, add half a ladle of batter and swirl it around to cover the bottom of the pan. Flip to cook the other side once the underneath is golden. Repeat until all the batter is used up.

 Take one pancake. And then another. And then another.

Starting with the lily that needs no gilding: sugar and lemon juice. It's a classic for good reason.

The problem is, pancakes being pancakes, they suit a lot of other ingredients beyond the lily that needs no gilding, such as chocolate and berry compote and ice cream and cream generally. Hundreds and thousands, maple syrup and butterscotch all have their place in the league table. And why not? Some days we eat apples because they're good for us, other days it's some crazy-name ice cream melting inside a hot golden pancake.

So, without further ado, some top sweet pancake fillings:

Cinnamon-and-sugar-coated apple slices fried in butter, topped with toasted walnuts, pecans or hazelnuts if you like.

Berry compote or cherry spooning sauce (see recipe on page 120).

Fresh berries, sprinkled with sugar.

Chocolate spread or Nutella, topped with sliced banana and – it has to be – some whipped cream.

All of the above will sing with some very good vanilla ice cream melting across the top.

Halloween

As the clocks change and we head in to the darker days of autumn and towards winter, children's endless fascination with all things spooky and love of all things sickly-sweet collide on Halloween.

So hang up your bats and spiders, dust down your cape — the trick-or-treaters are at large. Make sure you've got your hollowed-out pumpkin lit on the doorstep by dusk and be ready with your basket of goodies, because you're about to be visited by an array of tiny witches, skeletons and Draculas. In my experience, there's a rush of activity from 5.30 p.m. and it's all over in a couple of hours, once the ghouls have done their worst and have headed home for bed.

 ### Easy home-made sweets for the trick-or-treaters

Dip and coat marshmallows in melted milk or white chocolate, then sprinkle with hundreds and thousands. Leave to set on a sheet of baking parchment.

To make chocolate peanut butter cornflakes, heat a good tablespoonful of peanut butter with 100g milk chocolate in a heat-proof bowl over a pan of simmering water. When they are melted and blended, gently fold in cornflakes until they are well coated but not gloopy. Spoon in to small clusters and leave to set on baking parchment, or in small cupcake cases.

Bonfire Night

Bonfire Night is a beacon in the gloom of the British autumn and always makes me wonder why we don't all get together more often on these dark nights. The bonhomie is overflowing, the children love it and a good time is had by one and all (apart from cats and dogs and probably lots of other small furry creatures in hutches and woodland up and down the land).

In most places, it's a relatively straightforward night, ranging from Dad setting off a few rockets in the garden to big public displays. Everyone gets wrapped up, says a few oohs and ahhs and, after a while, goes home again. But not in Lewes.

I don't know how to begin when it comes to describing what happens to the usually peaceful town where I live on Bonfire Night. Dating back hundreds of years, it's a story of bonfire societies, elaborate costumes, huge processions, spectacular firework displays, effigies, thousands of visitors, barricades and lots and lots of very loud bangs for about 24 hours. Then on 6 November everything goes back to normal, and the bloke that yesterday was dressed as a Roman centurion and carrying a flaming torch through the streets is serving you in the bank.

Whatever you have planned for Bonfire Night, there's always the important matter of eating. Wherever you are, you need easy food that people can eat at different times as they come and go. The only given is that sausages must feature. So, here we have a recipe for hearty bangers and mash, to be eaten round the table or by the bowlful outside, with some old-fashioned toffee apples or brandy snaps to follow.

I like ginger beer to drink on Bonfire Night. Once upon a time, it was a freezing cold night when everyone got wrapped up in hats and gloves and what was needed was something to heat you through. Nowadays, it can be pretty mild and I think ginger beer is a good call — children like it, it's a bit different, and for the grown-ups a shot of gin livens things up nicely. Just don't confuse whose glass is whose.

Bill's bangers and parsley mash with onion gravy

SERVES 6

Preheat the oven to 180°C/160°C fan/gas mark 4.

Place the sausages on a baking tray with a tiny drizzle of oil. Don't prick them. Bake for 30-40 minutes until they are cooked and golden.

While the sausages are baking, boil the potatoes as you would normally for mash and get going on the gravy.

Melt the butter in a saucepan over a low heat, add the onions and fry slowly until they are golden brown and caramelized, at least 15 minutes. When they are soft and golden, stir in the thyme and cook for another minute or so. Sprinkle the flour over and stir to coat everything. Slowly add the wine, stirring as you go, and simmer to reduce the liquid by half. Add the stock, stir well, cover and simmer over a low heat for 15 minutes. Add the balsamic vinegar, season and keep warm over a low heat until needed.

By now the potatoes should be nearly cooked, so it's time to melt the butter gently in a small pan, add the garlic and cook until soft but not coloured. Add the milk and simmer quietly for 3-4 minutes. Turn off the heat and add the parsley.

When the potatoes have finished cooking, drain and put them through a potato ricer*, if you have one, or otherwise mash as usual. Gradually beat in the milk mixture to make a creamy mash.

Then it's on to big plates or, better still, in to bowls. Pile in the mash first, making a bit of a plateau for the sausages, then pour over a good ladleful of the gravy. Some wilted greens alongside – cavolo nero or cabbage – would be very good. Or just straight bangers and mash.

* A potato ricer makes all the difference to the consistency of mashed potatoes. Treat yourself.

12 good-quality sausages

FOR THE GRAVY

a generous knob or two of butter
3 large onions, finely sliced
a couple of sprigs of fresh thyme,
  roughly chopped
  (or 1 tsp dried thyme)
1 tbsp plain flour
150ml red wine
500ml vegetable stock
2 tbsp balsamic vinegar

FOR THE MASH

1kg Maris Piper or other good
  mashing potatoes, peeled
  and cut in chunks
50g butter
2 garlic cloves, peeled
  and crushed
100ml milk
a large handful of flat-leaf
  parsley, roughly chopped

Bonfire Night brandy snaps

It's Grandad's birthday on 5 November — my kids' grandad, that is. Poor bloke, he's pretty much a prisoner in his own home on Bonfire Night, right in the middle of the town. No chance of going out to a restaurant or even to the pub for a drink, so we all go round to his house and people come and go and it's like a port in the storm as the bangs and fireworks rain down outside.

And we always have brandy snaps. Old-fashioned, lacy, gingery brandy snaps filled with cream. So here's the recipe. They're relatively easy to make — the fiddly bit is the shaping and filling that follows — just remember to give them plenty of space while they're in the oven and get to the shaping soon after they come out.

Orange cream brandy snaps

MAKES 15–20

Preheat the oven to 180°C/160°C fan/gas mark 4.

Stir the butter, sugar, golden syrup and lemon juice in a pan over a moderate heat until the butter has melted and all the sugar has dissolved. Remove from the heat and stir in the flour and ginger, mixing to a smooth paste.

Once the mixture is completely cool, roll in to walnut-sized balls. Press them on to a greased tray, spacing them well apart as they will spread.

Bake for 5–7 minutes, until golden brown and lacy. Allow them to relax for a second or two, then mould them in to a tube shape by gently wrapping them round the handle of a wooden spoon. If they cool before you can mould them, put them back in the oven for a minute to soften again.

Whip the double cream and gently fold in the icing sugar, orange flower water and orange zest. Shortly before serving, put the cream in a large piping bag and fill each brandy snap. Stack them, Jenga-style, on a plate and serve immediately, while they're chewy and crispy.

125g unsalted butter
125g light soft brown sugar
125g golden syrup
4 tsp lemon juice
125g plain flour, sifted
1 tsp ground ginger

FOR THE CREAM
600ml double cream
1 tbsp icing sugar
1 tbsp orange flower water
the zest of 1 orange

Toffee apples

Wash and dry the apples, then push a wooden skewer, twig or wooden fork in to the stalk end and set to one side.

Put the sugar in a heavy-based pan with 100ml of water and cook for 5 minutes over a low heat. Do not be tempted to stir yet, as the sugar will crystallize if you do. When the sugar has completely dissolved, stir in the vinegar and golden syrup and bring to the boil.

If you have a sugar thermometer, boil to 140°C or the 'hard crack' stage, then remove the pan from the heat. If you don't have a sugar thermometer, when you think you're nearly there, remove the pan from the heat and drop a little of the toffee mixture in a glass of cold water. If it goes brittle, it's ready to coat the apples. If it stays soft, return the pan to the heat and continue to cook.

When the toffee is ready, dip each apple in and twist it round to coat it, lift it out and allow the excess to drip off. Place the apples on lightly oiled parchment paper and leave for an hour or so for the toffee to harden.

8 Cox's or any other
  crisp apples
400g golden caster sugar
1 tsp vinegar
4 tbsp golden syrup

Darker, colder days mark the beginning of winter.

Late autumn can be a mixed bag of sparkling blue skies and soggy grey ones, days for clearing the garden and days for staying in by the fire. And slowly it happens that beautiful, bountiful autumn inevitably tips towards winter, and you know what that means... the hungry months.

WINTER

The Hungry Months

What about winter, then? We never know what it's going to throw our way, and that's as it should be. However it blows — snowed-in days, wet and gloomy skies or bright sparkling blue walking-over-the-hills weekends — winter always lasts just that bit longer than we'd hoped and we all have to dig deep to keep smiling.

It has its moments, of course, lots of them. A frosty morning is always a thing of glory if you're well rugged up, and so too is a roaring fire when you get home from a long day's work. And, obviously, there are Christmas and New Year, sparkling like jewels at the end of December.

On the produce front, when you're stocking and shopping locally and seasonally, these are the hungry months: not too bad till Christmas, but then pretty tight through till March and April. And, as seasonal and local is how we operate at Bill's, things can start to look pretty sparse come February.

This is the time when canny cooks win the day, rustling up warming winter dishes from a bit of this, a bit of that and a creative scan of what's in the larder. These are the days for winter soups and stews packed with roots, grains and pulses, sweet citrusy puddings and cakes, feisty raw vegetable salads, and treats, lots of them, in the shape of spiced-up festive goodies, slow roasts and sticky puddings.

These are also the days for winter walks, out and about with friends and family, then all back for a long, lazy lunch that's been slowly roasting away in the oven. Easy food for happy times, so when you get asked how your weekend was, you can say 'Pretty good, actually'.

Bill's

WINTER CHAMPIONS

Stay warm, stay nourished and stay cheerful with the fresh, colourful and vitamin–packed produce that sees us through the darkest months.

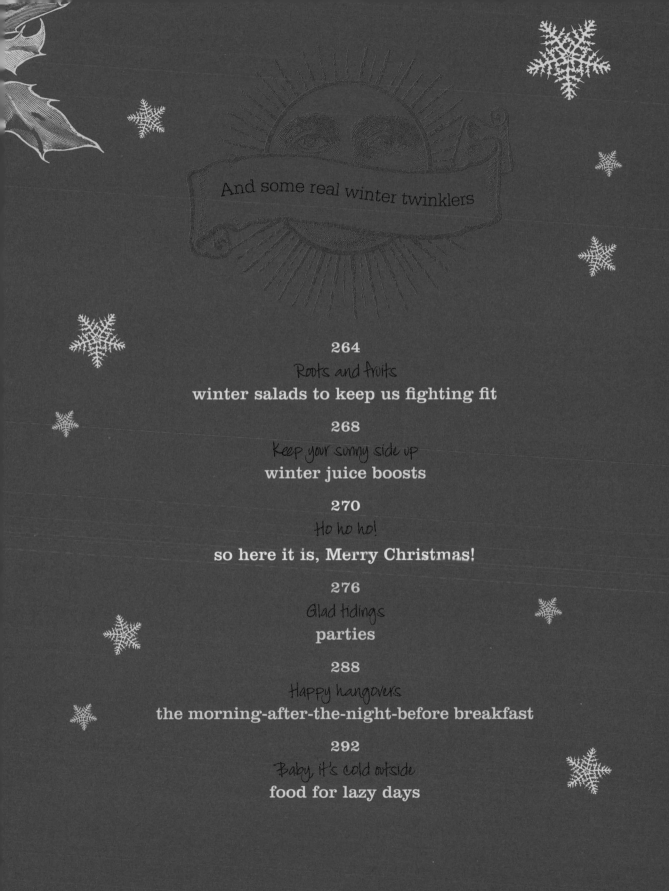

And some real winter twinklers

Purple sprouting broccoli
Midwinter star

With fresh leafy greens a bit thin on the ground, especially towards the dog-end of winter, purple sprouting broccoli is welcomed in to the store like a long-lost relative and it may quietly wonder what all the fuss is about. And although it's not what you would call a thing of beauty, it does deliver a whoop of superfood flavour and texture, is pretty versatile and there's no waste.

Steamed and stir-fried, purple sprouting broccoli goes with all sorts of fish and meat and is great in the classic Italian combination of pasta, broccoli and anchovies. Recipes vary — some include raisins, others pine nuts and / or garlic — but it's the broccoli-anchovy combo that hits the spot.

Purple sprouting, especially the early, more slender stems, can be treated in much the same way as asparagus. It loves hollandaise sauce, poached eggs and Parmesan and will happily lie like sardines in a flan case topped up with a creamy savoury custard and smothered in cheese.

Crispy broccoli stems

With its crispy texture, this is definitely the way forward for purple sprouting broccoli. You can serve the stems just as they are with a bowl of hollandaise for dipping, but they also sit very well on top of a bowl of creamy tagliatelle or a couple of golden apple and potato rösti (see recipe on page 175), or alongside grilled fish.

To prepare, trim away the woodier part of the stems if necessary and put the broccoli in a bowl with a little olive oil and sea salt. Toss them around, spread them on a baking tray and blast in a hot oven (200°C/180°C fan/gas mark 6) until crispy, 5-10 minutes, tops.

Border patrol pizza

Pizza is a clever way to get children to eat all types of vegetables. With a bready base, tomato sauce and plenty of cheese on top, you should be able to smuggle at least a few bits of greenery past the border patrol.

If you don't want to make the base, use a mix. Likewise the tomato sauce, though home-made is easy: blitz canned tomatoes till smooth, pour in a saucepan, add a teaspoon of sugar for each large can of tomatoes, a good tablespoonful of tomato purée, some dried herbs and seasoning, then let things simmer away on the hob until the sauce has reduced and thickened.

Oven roast any veg you think might stand a chance, including purple sprouting broccoli, squash, onions, peppers and carrots. Steam some kale if you have any. Layer all the veg on to the pizza, sprinkle generously with grated cheese and bake in a hot oven (200°C/180° fan/gas mark 6) until the base is cooked through and the cheese is golden and bubbling, around 15 minutes.

Serve, looking nonchalant.

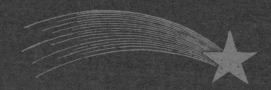

Winter greens
Of cabbages and (January) kings

You have to love a good brassica — the rich green of the leaves, the texture, the squeaky scrunching sound that a sharp knife makes as it slices through the middle. Then there is the variety: the sparkling fresh crunch of a January King, the gradation of greens when you slice open a Savoy, the frond-like beauty of cavolo nero, the sweeter, silkier bite of chard. And let's not forget red cabbage — raw and crunchy or cooked and sweetly soft.

Flavour, texture, big winter hitters

Raw, cabbage can be mixed with other vegetables, some oil and a spoonful or two of mayonnaise to make coleslaw; or added to salads and pitta bread fillings; or thrown in to soups at the last minute.

Cooked, whether it's steamed or stir-fried (go easy on the boiling), it's good with cheese, ham, game, bacon, pasta and noodles. A poached egg on top of a bowl of sautéed potatoes and cabbage makes a delicious, cheap and quick supper. Add some pancetta and it's fit for a king.

Even kale – not everyone's star vegetable – starts to take on a bit of a glow when shredded and stir-fried with some onion, chilli flakes, garlic and bacon.

Red cabbage, chopped and layered in an ovenproof dish with some sliced apples, a knob or two of butter and a sprinkle of salt and pepper, then covered tightly with a lid or some foil, will happily cook alongside a roast in the oven. Just take it out and stir it when the roast is done for a glossy infusion of flavour and colour.

Thai-style bubble and squeak

Obviously bubble and squeak — thrifty and homely, yet such a big savoury wonder —
has to feature in a book where the words crispy and golden are revered so highly.
And this version is like the girl in the film who takes off her glasses and shakes out
her golden tresses: surprisingly glamorous.

To create this exotic variation on a theme, you need some leftover greens (cabbage,
cavolo nero, kale etc.) and mashed potato — who would have thought the words 'leftover',
'mashed' and 'potato' could appear in the same sentence as 'exotic'? Or you can start
from scratch with fresh vegetables — it is worth it.

MAKES 6–8 PATTIES

Prepare the lemongrass stalk for the patties by cutting
away the tough top, the woody outer leaves and the very
bottom of the bulb along with any roots. Lightly bash
the inner pale yellow stalk with the blunt edge of a
heavy knife (to help release the oils), then chop very
finely. Gently fry the lemongrass, ginger and chilli in
a tablespoon of oil, add the spring onions and cook
for 2 more minutes until golden. Add the chopped
coriander and allow it to wilt before taking the pan
off the heat.

Put the wilted greens, the mashed potato and the
ingredients from the frying pan in a large bowl and
combine well. Season, shape in to 6–8 flatish patties
and dust with seasoned flour. Heat the other tablespoon
of oil in the pan and fry the patties until golden
(roughly 3 minutes each side).

Prepare the lemongrass stalks for the sauce by
trimming and lightly bashing as before, then either
leave the bruised inner stalks whole or chop in large
chunks. Put the lemongrass in a pan with all the
other sauce ingredients and heat through very gently
for about 3 minutes. Remove the lemongrass
before serving.

Serve the bubble and squeak patties with a good
scattering of chopped coriander on top and the sauce
either spooned over or on the side for dipping.

1 stalk of lemongrass
1 thumbnail of fresh ginger,
  peeled and finely chopped
1 red chilli, deseeded and
  finely chopped
2 tbsp vegetable oil
4 spring onions, shredded in
  long strips
a good handful of fresh coriander,
  roughly chopped, plus more
  to garnish
approx. 250g wilted greens,
  roughly chopped
approx. 500g mashed potato
25g plain flour, seasoned,
  for dusting patties

FOR THE SAUCE
4 fat stalks of lemongrass
2 tsp shrimp paste
2 tsp palm sugar or demerara sugar
2 tbsp lime juice
8 tbsp coconut milk

Chestnuts

Cobbled streets, braziers, smog

A brown paper bag almost too hot to hold, bought from a guy huddled over a brazier and wearing fingerless gloves, used to be as far as we went with chestnuts. But over recent years, this little treasure has shaken off its Dickensian cloak and sidled shyly in to the kitchen.

On the Continent they are eaten much more widely, particularly in sweet dishes, but we're still a bit suspicious of all that marron glacé malarkey — it just doesn't quite suit our palates (rather like pumpkin pie). No, here the chestnut is mostly at home in a savoury dish, where it really has put its feet up in front of the fire. It's especially good in stuffings, both the texture and flavour working well with a range of other ingredients.

Brussels sprouts, chestnuts and pancetta

There is a particular affinity between chestnuts and green vegetables, especially Brussels sprouts and other members of the cabbage family. You can stop at sprouts and chestnuts or, like here, you can add an extra dimension with some pancetta.

SERVES 4

You don't want the sprouts to look too tidy, so cut them open a bit and then tear them in to different-sized pieces. Blanch in boiling water for 3 minutes, run under cold water to refresh and leave to drain.

Fry the pancetta in its own fat in a small frying pan until almost golden. Heat the olive oil in a large frying pan, add the sprouts, fresh thyme and a sprinkle of brown sugar and cook until the sprouts are beginning to caramelize and blacken on the outsides and at the edges. Add the garlic and chestnuts and stir with a wooden spoon for a few minutes, until the garlic is cooked and the chestnuts are hot.

Serve warm with some crusty bread.

500g Brussels sprouts, cleaned and trimmed
125g pancetta, cut in 2cm cubes
1 tbsp olive oil
2 sprigs of fresh thyme
brown sugar, for sprinkling
2 garlic cloves, peeled and thinly sliced
200g chestnuts, vacuum-packed or roasted fresh
crusty bread, to serve (optional)

===================

To roast fresh chestnuts, start by buying slightly more than the recipe requires. Make slits in each chestnut with a sharp knife and roast them in a hot oven (200°C/180°C fan/gas mark 6) for about 25 minutes. When they are cool enough to handle, peel the outer and inner layers off.

===================

Ginger

Spice trail

Warming, soothing, aromatic ginger is one of the many ingredients that has transformed how we cook, helping us along the path to broader culinary horizons and repertoires. Powdered ginger has been a feature in British cooking for centuries, used in sweet puddings, biscuits and cakes — and ginger beer of course, but the fresh rhizome is something else again.

A staple of the supporting cast of ingredients we regularly use in our kitchens, fresh ginger adds a touch of the exotic to any dish it graces, bringing with it heat and flavour. Curries, stir-fries, soups and dhal, in it goes to add that spike of Eastern aromatics, working with other ingredients, particularly chilli, to round out the taste.

Spiced apple and ginger warmer

Good for weary, coldy days. Especially comforting when you're chilled to the bone.

The key ingredient here is the fresh ginger, grated or thinly sliced, to which you can add some or all of the following: orange and / or lemon slices, lemongrass, cinnamon, cloves, star anise, cardamom. Whatever you use, make sure you have about 500ml of liquid. Once your warmer is made, the pan can sit on the back of the hob all day and be heated through for topping up as you need it.

SERVES 2

Heat all the ingredients together very gently in a small pan for 10 minutes, to let all the flavours infuse. Allow to cool a little and then — and this part makes all the difference — pour through a strainer in to the most beautiful glasses you have. Moroccan tea glasses are perfect. Hold delicately and sip for instant soothing of the stylish variety.

500ml apple juice
1 large thumb of fresh ginger, sliced
1 slice of lemon
1 star anise
2 cardamom pods, split open
1 stalk of lemongrass (7-8cm long), trimmed and bruised

Butternut squash and coconut curry

Sweet and mild, creamy and comforting, this is a dish that allows ginger to really show what it brings to the table, sitting beautifully alongside the other flavours while adding its own character too. This recipe also works well using a medium-sized pumpkin instead of the butternut squash — just check after 15-20 minutes roasting time to see how it is getting along.

If you want the full curry experience, serve this with basmati or jasmine rice, poppadoms or prawn crackers, a spoonful of tamarind or mango chutney or a drizzle of sweet chilli sauce. A scattering of golden fried onions completes the look.

SERVES 4-6

Preheat the oven to 180°C/160°C fan/gas mark 4.

Put the butternut squash chunks in a large roasting tray, drizzle with sunflower oil and sprinkle with the cinnamon and coriander. Mix well with your hands to make sure the squash is well coated with the oil and spices. Season with salt and freshly ground black pepper, then bake in the oven for 20-25 minutes or until tender. Remove and set aside to cool.

While the squash is baking, you can get on with the sauce. Prepare the lemongrass by cutting away the tough top, the woody outer leaves and the very bottom of the bulb along with any roots. Lightly bash the inner pale yellow stalk with the blunt edge of a heavy knife (to help release the oils) and then chop very finely.

Heat 2 tablespoons of sunflower oil in a large frying pan and fry the shallots and ginger for 4-5 minutes over a medium heat, stirring occasionally, until slightly caramelized. Add the turmeric, garlic and lemongrass, stir well and cook for a further 2 minutes. Add two-thirds of the coriander along with the chilli, pineapple juice and 150ml of water. Bring to a simmer and allow to reduce by a third.

Liquidize the reduced sauce together with the coconut milk and a quarter of the cooked butternut squash, and transfer to a large saucepan. Add the fish sauce, stir in the remaining squash along with the spinach, sugar and water chestnuts and simmer on a low heat for 10 minutes.

To serve, garnish with the remaining coriander and some salt and pepper cashew nuts.

1 large or 2 small butternut squash (approx. 1.2kg), peeled, deseeded and cut in bite-sized chunks

2 tbsp sunflower oil, plus extra for drizzling

1 tsp ground cinnamon

1 tsp ground coriander

3 stalks of lemongrass

3 shallots, finely chopped

2 thumbs of fresh ginger, peeled and finely chopped

½ tsp finely chopped fresh turmeric or 1 tsp ground turmeric

2 garlic cloves, peeled and finely chopped

1 small bunch of fresh coriander, finely chopped

1 medium red chilli, with or without seeds, finely chopped

225ml pineapple juice

1 x 400ml tin of coconut milk

2 tbsp Thai fish sauce

200g fresh spinach

2 tsp palm sugar or demerara sugar

1 x 150g tin of water chestnuts, drained and sliced

salt and pepper cashew nuts, to garnish

Salt and pepper cashew nuts

Toast 200g of cashew nuts in a medium oven (160°C/140°C fan/gas mark 3) for about 5 minutes until lightly golden. Drizzle with a tablespoon of olive oil and season with salt and pepper, give them a good shake to make sure they are all coated and then put them back in the oven for another minute. Keep an eye on them, though, and don't let them burn. Drain on kitchen paper and allow to cool.

These are great as a garnish and are also good with drinks or as part of a mezze plate (200g will serve 6-8 as a snack).

Cranberries

What a commotion

We break the rule for cranberries. They aren't local. They come from North America. But we have to have them because we love to cook with them, and so do our customers, and they are as much a part of Christmas as crackers.

Which is funny really, because when I was a kid we hadn't even heard of cranberries. But no Christmas table is complete without them nowadays and for this we thank Delia Smith, who introduced them in 1995 in her *Delia Smith's Winter Collection* book and television series. Yes, she caused a cranberry commotion. And since then they have taken pride of place on the table, which is a bit like the newest recruit to the football team deciding they are going to be captain. But no matter, we forgive and welcome them for the shot of colour and tart berry zing they bring to the party. But only because it's Christmas.

The word 'remarkable' is often bandied around when talking about the health-giving properties of cranberries, so the more clever ways we can think of including them in our diet, the better.

Scatter a handful of dried berries on your granola or across salads and fruit salads, or mix in to couscous. Fresh cranberries can also be added to tagines and lamb or chicken stews — just a handful or two near the end of the cooking time.

Cranberry Sauce

Cranberry sauce is very good in place of chutney with roast chicken and in sandwiches. It can also be combined with other fruit to use in crumbles and pies or mixed with mincemeat for filling mince pies to soften the flavour and add colour.

This will make a good couple of bowlfuls, so you can bottle some to store in the fridge for up to a week. You can keep it really simple — cranberries and orange juice — or you can fancy it up a bit and add any or all of the following: star anise, cinnamon, vanilla, port, brandy, sugar, chopped orange or apple. Let's say we choose fancy:

Put the sugar, orange juice and 4 tablespoons of the port in a medium-sized pan and heat gently until the sugar has dissolved. Stir in the cranberries, orange zest, apple and cinnamon stick and simmer gently for about 10 minutes with the lid off, until the fruit is soft. Stir in the last tablespoonful of port, remove from the heat and allow to cool a little.

Best dish, best spoon.

175g caster sugar
the zest and juice of 1 orange
5 tbsp port
approx. 250g cranberries, fresh or defrosted from frozen
1 eating apple, cored and finely chopped
a small piece of cinnamon stick

If you insist

Leftover cranberry sauce is just the best addition to Christmastime sandwiches, as it really does sit perfectly with all those delicious bits and pieces that beckon from the fridge surprisingly soon after eating one of the year's most filling dinners: turkey, stuffing, sausage meat, Brie, Camembert, blue cheese, goat's cheese, yes please, go on then, if you insist. Maybe not all of them in the one sandwich, but there again…

Pomegranates

Rubies, coronet, red carpet now please

Like an exotic princess, the pomegranate sweeps in with an enormous sense of occasion, demanding that we take in every little detail. For a start, the colour: not quite red or orange or yellow or even pink, but rather a blended hue of them all. And then there's that jaunty little coronet perched on top (though it's actually the bottom). All this before you even open it up to reveal those gorgeous ruby-red jewels packed tightly inside.

Scatter is the word to use with pomegranate seeds, across a real array of foods, both savoury and sweet: salads, humous, fish dishes, stir-fries, pizza, fruit salads, cakes, trifles, yoghurt, and anything involving couscous, mint, rosewater or chocolate. Honestly, all of these and more will thank you, as those little red seeds deliver a real whoop of midwinter goodness and colour every time.

Sprinkled over at the last moment, they add a sharp fruitiness that is the perfect foil for anything fatty or rich, while blander milky dishes, such as porridge and rice pudding, especially love them. After all, we eat with our eyes as well as our mouths, so the splash of colour and then the tart/sweet burst of flavour lifts dishes like these and transforms them in to something much more interesting.

Three risqué ways with a pomegranate

I know of three ways to eat a pomegranate, though there may well be others.

1. Cup it in both hands and gently but firmly massage and squeeze the whole fruit until you can almost feel through to the other side. Pierce it and suck out the juice.

2. Cut it in half across the middle. Then whack the skin with a wooden spoon and shoot the seeds in to a bowl. This should remove most of them.

3. Cut it open and gently tease it apart, so you can eat the fruit in clusters, avoiding the pith as it's very bitter.

Bringing with them, as they do, a sense of occasion, pomegranates do well at parties. Have a look at recipes for pomegranate and beetroot ripple ice cream (page 284) and pomegranate and orange juice cocktails (page 276).

Oranges

Navel gazing

Oranges take centre stage in January as, right on cue, the season delivers just what's needed for a midwinter boost of vitamins (one orange supplies over 100% of our daily requirement of vitamin C), colour, flavour and dancing senoritas from Seville.

Do we love them enough? Or do we take them a bit for granted, what with them always being there? When did you last sit down, peel an orange and eat it, bursting-with-flavour segment by bursting-with-flavour segment? If it was in the last week, you may go home early. If not, try it. That's all I'm saying.

Orange Wednesdays... and Thursdays, Fridays, Saturdays

Add orange segments to just about any salad. Coleslaws, in particular, and salads featuring watercress. Couscous, mint, feta and orange is a very good mix of textures and flavours too.

Put a big bowl of orange segments on the table to eat during and after fish and chips, burgers and take aways. Especially good with children who naturally gravitate towards the fresh zing of the fruit.

And finally

For fancy, squeeze blood orange juice in to champagne or sparkling wine.

For thrifty, boil the peel in sugared water to make candied peel for cakes.

For lift, add orange juice to soups at the last moment – especially good with carrots and tomatoes.

Sunburst glories

What a beautiful fruit a blood orange is. Right in the gloomiest middle of winter, nature rolls this little jewel on to the table. It is definitely one of my top five fresh produce moments. No forcing, just totally in season, though only for a short while — from the back end of January till early March.

Slice across to get the full sunburst glory and layer on to salads, cakes, yoghurt and fish. Which says quite a bit for how versatile they are!

See the recipe on page 266 for a textured winter salad starring blood oranges.

Oh, you darling clementines

Keeping us topped up with fresh doses of vitamin C, big bowlfuls of clementines or satsumas on the kitchen table, and one in everyone's lunchbox, should be the habit in homes from sea to shining sea right through the winter, till we shout, as one, 'Enough already of the small orange things', by which time spring should be peeping round the corner and we'll have made it.

Remember tangerines? It were the pips what done for them. Remember tinned mandarins with evaporated milk for pudding? Anyone? OK, not to worry, but it was actually quite a nice treat if you were eleven and your mum had said 'No pudding tonight' and then magicked a couple of tins out of the larder to stop you looking so disappointed. That's Mother Love.

Sweet citrus-scented Sevilles

Dads like marmalade. Or at least Dads in old films like it. They sit at the table, legs crossed, reading their newspaper and speaking authoritatively on important matters. And they're often eating marmalade on toast. It's all very British, in a clipped and bygone sort of way. Then they rush off to catch the train.

And so, come January, when the Seville oranges are in the shops for those few short weeks, in the time-honoured way, cooks across the land put on their pinnies, dust off their preserving pans, pull out their favourite marmalade recipe and fill the house with the sweet citrus scent of oranges bubbling away on the hob.

You can ring the changes if you feel the need by adding other citrus fruit or stem ginger, or a few glugs of whisky or rum, then bottle it up, write the labels and take a few moments to admire your handiwork before getting the bread in the toaster and putting the kettle on.

Of course, you could just nip to the shops and buy some, but then you don't get to dance round the kitchen with your wooden spoon raised above your head, swishing your pinny and stamping along to loud Flamenco music.*

* Bill's marmalades are good, though, and you do get the pretty labels. It's a tough call.

Seville and blood orange marmalade

Place one or two saucers in the freezer as you will need these to test for a set.

Put oranges and lemons in a large heavy-based pan, ideally a preserving pan if you have one. Pour in the water, cover the pan with tin foil and bring to the boil. Simmer gently for 1½-2 hours until the fruit is very soft.

Remove the fruit from the pan with a slotted spoon and, when it is cool enough to handle, halve and scrape out all the seeds and pith. Place them in the middle of a large piece of muslin, tie it up in a secure bundle and place back in the poaching liquid.

Slice the softened fruit skins in thin or thick shreds, however you like them, and put them in the poaching liquid too. Add the star anise, and boil for 10 minutes. Remove the muslin bag and continue to boil until you've reduced the liquid by about a third.

Take the preserving pan off the heat, making sure it's off the boil as you mustn't let the sugar crystallize, then stir in the sugar. Add the juice from the blood oranges and bring the marmalade back to the boil, stirring to make sure all the sugar has dissolved. Boil rapidly for about 10-15 minutes.

Test for a set by placing a teaspoon of the marmalade on a cold saucer from the freezer. If the mixture thickens and forms a skin that wrinkles when you push it with your finger, then it is ready. If not, carry on boiling for a further 10 minutes and test again.

When the marmalade has reached setting point and is ready, turn off the heat and leave for 15 minutes. Remove any scum that may have accumulated on the top, remove the star anise if you like (though I think it's nice to leave it in) and then decant the marmalade in to sterilized jars.

1.5kg Seville oranges, washed and scrubbed
2 lemons, washed and scrubbed
3.6 litres of water
4 star anise
1.5kg golden granulated sugar
1.5kg soft brown sugar
the juice of 3 blood oranges

To sterilize jars, wash them in hot soapy water, rinse and shake off the excess water. Put them on a baking tray in a low oven for 10 minutes. Alternatively, you can run them through a hot wash in a dishwasher.

Marmalade peanut flapjacks

I don't think I need to tell you how delicious these are going to be.
You can just tell – flapjacks, but with peanuts and marmalade. I know.

MAKES 12
(OR MORE, DEPENDING HOW SMALL YOU CUT THEM)

Preheat the oven to 180°C/160°C fan/gas mark 4.
Lightly butter a 20 x 20cm (or equivalent capacity) tin.

Gently melt the butter in a large saucepan and add
the sugar, marmalade, honey and peanut butter.
Stir and heat slowly until everything is melted together.
Remove from the heat and mix in the whole peanuts,
oats and orange zest.

Tip the mixture in to the buttered tin, make sure it's
evenly distributed and press down, smoothing the top.
Bake for 20 minutes until golden.

Leave to cool for 5-10 minutes and then cut in to squares
or rectangles, but don't try to take the flapjack out of the
tin until it's completely cooled. Stored in an airtight tin,
they will keep for several days.

225g butter
30g soft brown sugar
30g coarse cut marmalade
40g runny honey
50g crunchy peanut butter
50g roasted natural peanuts
350g porridge oats
the zest of 1 orange

Marmalade-glazed ham

Sweet and savoury, sticky and crackly – all thanks to a few spoonfuls of marmalade. If you're not sure how big a ham to get, as a rough guide, a 2.5kg boneless ham or a 3kg bone-in ham feeds about 8 people.

Boil the ham in enough water to cover it, skimming occasionally to get rid of any scum that collects on the top. You can throw in a couple of bay leaves, some carrots and celery sticks, a star anise or two, pink peppercorns and maybe some juniper berries to boil with the ham, if you would like to spice things up a bit. Once it is cooked through (30 minutes per 500g should do it), remove from the heat and allow to cool in the broth (which you can keep to use for soups).

Once the ham is cool enough to handle, put it on a board and cut off the rind and some of the fat, leaving just a thin layer – 12mm at most. Score the ham in diamond shapes and decorate with cloves for a festive feel, before putting it in an ovenproof dish, ready to glaze.

Preheat the oven to 200°C/180°C fan/gas mark 6. Tip half a jar of your favourite marmalade in a pan and gently heat, then brush all over the ham. Put the glazed ham in the oven and baste every 10 minutes or so until it is crusty and golden (about 20 minutes). I like it overcooked, almost burned. Take it out of the oven and leave to cool.

Great, perfect even, with coleslaw and a jacket potato. Very good in sandwiches. And did someone mention poached eggs?

Roots and fruits

Winter salads to keep us fighting fit

First in to save the day, when we start thinking that winter is the time for roly-poly waistlines and not for big nutrient-rich, bug-busting salads, are roots — roasted until they're sweet and sticky — and fruit, most often citrus, but also apples, pears and dried fruit.

Simple, colourful bowls of health-giving fresh produce, combined with swashbuckling dressings, provide us with the big energy and flavour hits we all need at this time of year. Keep mixing it up and being creative: surprise your palate with grapefruit segments, roast parsnips, caramelized onions, crunchy slivers of fennel or cabbage. A big plateful of raw fruit and veg every day will help you to motor through the winter.

Midwinter coleslaw

Coleslaw should be your default winter salad. You can eat this on its own or it's good alongside a sandwich or quiche. Alternatively you could load some on to a just-baked potato and grate some Cheddar cheese over the top to turn it in to a meal.

SERVES 6

Mix the mayonnaise, crème fraîche, mustard, lemon zest and lemon juice together in a small bowl and season well.

Roughly chop the cabbage and discard the stems. Peel and roughly grate the parsnip and the celeriac, immediately tossing the grated celeriac in lemon juice to stop it going brown. Put the cabbage, parsnip, celeriac and parsley in a large bowl, pour over the dressing and gently combine. Taste and season again if necessary, then scatter the seeds over the top.

4 tbsp mayonnaise
2 tbsp crème fraîche
3 tsp Dijon mustard
the zest of half a lemon
2 tbsp lemon juice, plus more
  for the celeriac
half a Savoy cabbage
1 parsnip
half a celeriac
a handful of parsley, chopped
crunchy munchy seeds
  (see recipe on page 39)

Wintergreen salad

This isn't a stand-alone salad: it works best as a great winter vitamin boost alongside other dishes — more salads or some lamb chops or white fish. Make sure you let it stand before serving, as that allows the kale to wilt in the lemon juice and the flavours to grow.

SERVES 4–6

Cut the kale in very thin ribbons and put them in a salad bowl, leaving any thicker stems to go in the compost. Whisk the lemon juice and olive oil together, then pour over the kale strips. Toast the pine nuts by dry-fying them in a small pan for a minute or two, keeping an eye on them to make sure they don't burn, then add them with the cheese to the dressed kale. Combine gently and leave to stand for a good hour before serving.

200g kale
the juice of 2 lemons
50ml good olive oil
50g pine nuts
60g Pecorino or
    Parmesan shavings

Orange, watercress and fennel salad

To make this dish more substantial, you can add some beans or pulses. Soya beans work particularly well — you can buy them (also called edamame) fresh, frozen or dried. If you use dried, you'll need to soak them in advance. Cook the fresh or soaked beans in boiling water for 10 minutes (3 minutes if using frozen beans) until tender, then drain and set aside to cool until you are putting the salad together.

SERVES 4

Use a peeler to cut the celery in strips. Twist each strip round your finger to curl it and place in iced water until needed.

To make the dressing, whisk the orange juice, yoghurt and olive oil together in a small jug and season with salt and freshly ground black pepper.

Arrange the fennel slices and watercress leaves in a large shallow bowl. Follow with the orange segments and the soya beans (if using). Drain the celery curls and sit them on top. Drizzle the dressing over the salad, scatter with the toasted pine nuts and serve immediately.

2 sticks of celery
1 large bulb fennel, thinly sliced
2 bunches of watercress, stems removed
1 large blood or navel orange, peeled and sliced in segments
50g soya beans (optional)
30g pine nuts, toasted

FOR THE DRESSING
2 tbsp orange juice
5 tbsp Greek yoghurt
2 tbsp olive oil

Keep your sunny side up

Winter juice boosts

With shorter days and not a lot of sunshine to go round, midwinter is the time when we really need to keep topping up with good doses of nutrients. Colourful, vitamin-packed juices will do the trick.

Carrot, orange and ginger

Time to get the juicer out. This is a top hitter at Bill's during the winter months. Sort of blows your head off, but in a nice way.

MAKES 2 TALL GLASSES

1 large thumb of fresh ginger
6 medium carrots, roughly chopped
the juice of 4 oranges

Peel and chop the root ginger as finely as possible. Juice the carrots and ginger together — ginger doesn't love juicing machines, but if you've chopped it finely, a good hit will make it through with the carrot juice. Add the freshly squeezed orange juice, stir and serve.

Beetroot and orange juice

Bring on the beetroot for its unbelievable colour at this time of year. You only have to look at it to know it's going to be good for you.

MAKES 2 GLASSES

Chop the beetroot in small chunks and run it through the juicer, adding the freshly squeezed juice from the oranges as you go to combine the two. Serve immediately.

1 medium beetroot, peeled
the juice of 3 oranges

Apple, parsley and lemon juice

As the rounds of winter parties take their toll, we all need a little something to make us feel healthy, revitalised and full of zing again.

MAKES 2 GLASSES

Put all ingredients in the blender and blitz. Drink straight away.

the juice of 3 apples
the juice of half a lemon
a handful of parsley

Ho ho ho!

We throw everything we can think of in to making Christmas at Bill's as festive and celebratory as we possibly can. Carol singers, jazz quartets, a bloke roasting chestnuts out the front, gingerbread men hanging from the rafters, big baskets of chocolate Santas, cheesy Christmas songs on a loop. Honestly, classy it isn't.

In the Lewes store it all gets going with Christmas Late Night Shopping, which takes place in the first week of December. All the shops in town stay open till about 9 p.m. and the staff hand out mulled wine and mince pies and, crucially, dress up in daft costumes. The residents of Lewes take to the streets and a good time is had by everyone.

Aly, who has worked with me since the beginning, likes nothing more than an opportunity to get dressed up and so every year she announces 'the theme' and all the waitresses then spend a lot of time discussing their outfits and the waiters do their best to wriggle out of working that night, which is fine because the girls are falling over themselves to dress up as fairies or characters from films or whatever Aly has decreed.

That evening launches our assault on Christmas, as it's our deadline to get all the Bill's hampers and Christmas goodies in to the stores, and we make things look really sparkly and off we go on the mad slalom that takes us through till Christmas Eve, when it all peaks and the place is packed with locals — there for a glass of mulled wine or a mug of hot chocolate, crammed in with piles of coats and bags and babies — them, their children, parents, friends and friends of friends, the sort of motley gathering you only ever get at Christmastime. Which is what it's all about. Take it away, Noddy.

Twinkle, twinkle, home-made gifts

Imagine if someone has gone to the trouble of making you some Turkish Delight for Christmas? Not buying a box, though I admit those Hazer Baba boxes are beautiful, but actually finding the recipe and buying the ingredients and getting all messed up with gelatine and icing sugar in the kitchen and choosing the right container and lining it with tissue paper and carefully placing the little cubes in and wrapping it all up. Then writing a label.

I mean, really, that's what I call a Christmas present. If someone gave that to me, I'd be made up. Of course, I'd make a show of bring chuffed to bits with the socks and DVDs too, but the home-made present would be the one to bring on the old Christmas glow.

The best bit about home-made and edible presents is that they can be very simple and quite often involve only a tiny bit of cooking. They mostly come down to sourcing and preparation and only part of it is to do with what's inside, as quite a lot of the *Ta Da*! comes from the packaging and decoration.

The list of what you can make is endless – from preserves and flavoured spirits to cakes and biscuits, sweets and savouries, and it's never too late for any of them. Even if something needs to sit for a while, you can just add a 'Not to be opened until...' label.

 Spicy nuts are easy to make as presents. Spread the nuts evenly on a baking tray – a handful or two each of almonds, Brazils, natural peanuts, hazelnuts – and roast in a medium oven (180°C/160°C fan/gas mark 4) for 5 minutes or so. Mix cayenne pepper, ground cumin, cinnamon and celery salt together in a small bowl. Take the nuts out of the oven, sprinkle with the spice mix, drizzle with olive oil and a tablespoon or two of honey and stir well to make sure they are all evenly coated. Put the tray back in the oven for a further 5-10 minutes, stirring once or twice and generally keeping an eye on the nuts to make sure they don't turn and burn in a moment. Once roasted, remove from the oven and leave to cool completely before spooning in to pretty jars or cellophane wraps held together with a ribbon tie.

Cinnamon stars

These stars, packed in crinkly cellophane, tied with some ribbon or raffia and given a pretty label, have got the whole 'jingle bell rocks' thing going on. They take a little time to make, as you need to rest the dough at a couple of stages, but you can use this time to deck the hall with boughs of holly. And you don't need to stick to star shapes — anything Christmassy or even little hearts will go down well.

MAKES 12 LARGE STARS OR 30–40 SMALLER ONES

Whisk the egg whites in a clean bowl with a pinch of salt and the lemon juice. Slowly add the icing sugar while continuing to whisk until stiff and glossy. Put one third of the mixture in a separate bowl for the topping, cover and refrigerate until needed.

Add 250g of the ground almonds (300g if you're using large egg whites), the cinnamon and the lemon zest to the remaining meringue. Fold in with a spatula until well blended (at this stage it's quite a wet mix). Cover with cling film and chill for 45 minutes.

Sprinkle the remaining 50g of ground almonds on a clean dry work surface and tip the chilled mixture on top. Knead for a couple of minutes to form a sticky dough and then roll out to a thickness of half a centimetre. Spread the remaining meringue mixture across the top with a palette knife and leave to dry for an hour.

Preheat the oven to 180°C/160°C fan /gas mark 4.

Dip a star cutter in cold water to minimize sticking and cut out as many star shapes as you can, placing them on baking sheets. In order to avoid wasting the off-cuts (which can't be re-rolled because of the meringue topping), you can always bake them too, either just as they are or put together in patchwork shapes. They won't make it as gifts — but they taste just as good. Bake for 8–10 minutes on the lowest shelf of the oven, until the biscuits are brown and the meringue is slightly golden. Remove from the oven, place on a wire rack and leave to cool.

Once they are cool, dust with a little icing sugar and/or cinnamon to decorate — and to stop them sticking together when packaged. You can then store them in a tin till you need them or bag them up straight away. Clear cellophane and lots of ribbon look lovely, especially if you have some edible stardust to sprinkle in the bag. Or a pretty box lined with coloured tissue paper also works well.

* If you are looking for something else to do with the leftover yolks, you could always make Shrewsbury biscuits (see recipe on page 66) or lemon curd (also page 66).

3 egg whites*
2 tbsp lemon juice
350g icing sugar,
  plus more to dust
300–350g ground
  almonds
  (depending on egg size)
1 tbsp ground cinnamon,
  plus more to dust
1 tsp lemon zest

Parties

And lo, it came to pass, that in a brief moment of seasonal bonhomie, you invited friends and neighbours round for a Christmas drink. And so now, when you're aching to do little more than lie on the sofa, and what you really ought to be doing is shopping and wrapping, you can't do either because you have to festoon your house, the ground floor at least, with twinkling lights and sprayed (by you) branches that have been decorated with home-made (by you) stars and angels. You also need to prepare a delicious selection of unusual canapés and trays of drinks and have a nice time and clear up afterwards.

But first, you'll be needing a drink.

Pomegranate and orange juice cocktails

Bright sunshiny red and full of bubbles, this is the drink to greet your guests with.
The non-alcoholic version — using sparkling white grape or apple juice instead of Prosecco — is good too.

MAKES 10 GLASSES

Using a citrus juicer, juice the oranges and pomegranates in two separate jugs, then put in the fridge to chill. When you are ready to serve the drinks, half fill the glasses with sparkling wine and top up with orange juice. Finish with a little swirl of pomegranate juice.

10 blood or navel oranges
2 pomegranates
2 bottles of Prosecco
  or other sparkling wine

Bill's Marvellous Mezze

There's a lot to be said for mezze. From dim sum to tapas, most cultures have their own interpretation and frankly the British equivalent was always a bit embarrassing. Cheese and pineapple on a stick, anyone? Happily, we waved goodbye to all that a while ago and in to the bin went sausage rolls and egg sandwiches, bowls of prawn cocktail crisps and soggy quiche.

And in swept the exotica: babaganoush and falafel, marinated olives and focaccia, guacamole and spiced almonds. Mezze, with all its colourful, flavourful glamour, was here to stay.

And when you're throwing a party, a bit of glamour is just what's required. The good thing is you only need to choose a few signature dishes and then quite ordinary bowls of carrot sticks or cherry tomatoes, toasted breads and clementines will bathe in their reflected glory. Turn each of the following dishes out in a colourful selection of bowls, platters, trays and baskets and tuck the food in among jugs of cutlery and candles on tall sticks, lanterns and fairy lights. Throw in some baubles and the odd cherub and your table will be ready to ding dong merrily on high.

I have to say the Bill's mezze plate is hard to beat. So here, for your delectation and delight, I'm sharing with you the recipes for each dish. You don't need to do all these dishes, just some will bring a whoop to the table. They're all easy, all yours. And as for hand-painted branches of stars, pah! Everyone will be so transfixed by the food, they'll forget to notice.

Babaganoush

SERVES 8-12

Preheat the oven to 180°C/160°C fan/gas mark 4.

Halve and score the aubergines, drizzle the cut surfaces with 2 tablespoons of olive oil, season with salt and a twist or two of black pepper and roast in the oven for 25 minutes, or until soft. Leave to cool.

Finely chop the pulp of one of the cooled aubergine halves. Scrape the pulp out of the other three halves and place in a food processor with 2 tablespoons of olive oil and the garlic, lemon juice, zest, crème fraîche, torn bread and tahini. Blend until smooth, then transfer to a bowl. Stir in the parsley and chopped aubergine, season to taste and drizzle with a little olive oil.

2 large aubergines
4 tbsp olive oil, plus extra
   for drizzling
2 smoked (or fresh)
   garlic cloves, peeled
   and chopped
the zest and juice of 1 lemon
80ml crème fraîche
3 slices of white bread,
   crusts removed
3 generous tbsp tahini
   (approx. 60g)
a handful of flat-leaf parsley,
   very finely chopped

Humous

SERVES 8-12

If you are using dried chickpeas, drain off the soaking water, put them in a pan and cover with fresh cold water. Add the bicarbonate of soda and cook for 1½-2 hours. When they have softened, drain and allow to cool. If you're using tinned chickpeas, drain and rinse them well.

Fry the onion and pepper in a tablespoon of oil until soft, then tip in to a blender. Add all the other ingredients apart from the chickpeas and pomegranate seeds, and blitz. Add a good three-quarters of the chickpeas and blend until smoothish but still a bit chunky. Transfer to a serving dish and mix the rest of the chickpeas in to the humous, and season well with salt and freshly ground black pepper. Top with a drizzle of olive oil, a dusting of paprika and a scattering of fresh pomegranate seeds.

2 x 400g tins of chickpeas
   or 350g dried chickpeas,
   soaked overnight
½ tsp bicarbonate of soda (for
   dried chickpeas only)
1 red onion, diced
1 red pepper, finely diced
6 tbsp olive oil, plus extra
   for drizzling
2 tsp smoked paprika, plus
   extra for dusting
1 tsp coriander seeds, ground
1 tsp cumin seeds, ground
3 garlic cloves, peeled and
   finely chopped
a big handful of fresh coriander,
   roughly chopped
the zest and juice of 1 lemon
2 tbsp sweet chilli sauce
3 tbsp tahini
pomegranate seeds, to garnish

Guacamole

Put three-quarters of the chopped avocado in a blender. Add the cumin, ground and fresh coriander, parsley and lemon and lime juices, and blend until smooth. Transfer the mixture to a bowl and stir in the onion, chilli, tomatoes and the rest of the chopped avocado. Season well with salt, freshly ground black pepper and Tabasco.

If you aren't eating it straight away, push the avocado stones in to the guacamole to stop it going brown, cover with cling film and refrigerate until you are ready to serve.

3 ripe Hass avocados, peeled,
  stoned and roughly chopped
½ tsp ground cumin
½ tsp ground coriander
a good handful of fresh
  coriander, roughly chopped
a good handful of flat-leaf
  parsley, roughly chopped
the juice of 1 lemon
the juice of 1 lime
1 red onion, finely diced
1 red chilli, deseeded and finely diced
4 medium tomatoes,
  deseeded and finely chopped
a dash of Tabasco sauce

Marinated olives

You don't need to worry about quantities for this dish, as long as there are far more olives than anything else. And you don't necessarily need all of the ingredients listed here, either. The main thing is to get the olives in to some olive oil for a good few hours — you want them well coated rather than swimming.

Roughly mix everything apart from the lime wedges together in a bowl, cover and leave to marinate for 3-4 hours. Decorate with the lime wedges to serve.

olives
pickled or fresh garlic
cornichons or
  finely chopped gherkin
mixed dried herbs
grated lemon zest
good olive oil
lime wedges

Potato, sweet potato and parsnip chips with three dips

Some small cheats in here, all in the name of enabling you to breeze through party preparations. Quite big cheats, actually – opening jars and adding to what's in them. While the chips are cooking, or earlier if you're trying to get ahead, prepare the dips.

SERVES 8-12

Preheat the oven to 200°C/180°C fan/gas mark 6.

Throw the chipped potatoes in a large, shallow roasting tin or two, making sure there'll be enough room to add the parsnips and sweet potatoes later. Drizzle with oil, season with sea salt and freshly ground black pepper and, using your hands, mix the chips around to ensure they are all coated in the oil. Place the tray in the oven and bake for 20 minutes.

Take the chips out of the oven and turn them, scraping any burnt bits off the bottom of the tin. Add the parsnips and sweet potatoes, mix them in and return the tin to the oven for a further 30 minutes.

When they're done – somewhat caramelized and blackened – remove from the oven and stack them in shallow dishes to serve.

5 large Desirée potatoes, skins on and cut in long chips

3-4 tbsp olive oil

5 parsnips, peeled and cut in long, slender chips

5 sweet potatoes, peeled and cut in chunky chips

Garlic mayo dip

Place the garlic cloves in a mortar with a pinch of sea salt and grind them to a paste with the pestle. Put the garlic in a mixing bowl with the mayonnaise and oil and stir to combine well, then transfer to a decorative bowl or dish. Cover with cling film and keep in the fridge until you're ready to serve the chips.

3 garlic cloves, peeled

200g good-quality mayonnaise

1 scant tbsp olive oil

Pesto and pine nut dip

Pour the pesto in an attractive dish and add the olive oil and three-quarters of the pine nuts. Stir well and garnish with the remaining pine nuts.

100g good-quality pesto

3 tbsp olive oil

50g pine nuts, toasted

Double chilli sauce

Pour the sweet chilli sauce in to a dipping bowl, add the other ingredients and give it all a good stir.

120ml sweet chilli sauce

1 red chilli, deseeded and finely chopped

the zest and juice of 1 lime

1 scant tbsp balsamic vinegar

Pomegranate and beetroot ripple ice cream

This will impress the guests and stop them quibbling about the fact that you haven't made a seasonal display out of pine cones and spun sugar. In fact, it will stop them in their tracks when you appear with a tray of shot glasses of the palest pink ice cream, ribboned through with a dark crimson thread of sweet beetroot purée.

You can roast the beetroot in advance if you're using the oven for something else. Or you can use home-made cranberry sauce (see recipe on page 249) or redcurrant relish (see page 115) for the ripple – as long as you have the colour contrast.

MAKES 12 SHOTS

Roast the beetroot on a baking tray, skin on, in a fairly hot oven (200°C/180°C fan/gas mark 6) until soft – roughly 30-45 minutes. Allow to cool before peeling. Purée the peeled beetroot in a blender, adding a little icing sugar if you feel it needs it (a tablespoonful or so should be enough).

Cut the pomegranates in half across the middle. Cover and store one half in the fridge until you come to serve, as you'll be using the seeds to decorate. Juice the other halves with a citrus juicer. Boil the juice in a small saucepan until reduced by half (to approximately 150ml) – it should have thickened slightly and become syrupy. Pour in to a large bowl and set aside to cool.

Stir the lime juice and zest, vanilla and icing sugar in to the cooled juice until the sugar dissolves. Add the cream and whip until it just begins to make soft peaks. Carefully spoon the mixture in to a plastic airtight container and gently fold the beetroot purée through to form ripples. Place in the freezer for 4-5 hours or, ideally, overnight.

To serve, scoop the ice cream in to shot glasses using a teaspoon, sprinkle each serving with a few pomegranate seeds and deliver to your guests, accepting compliments with grace.

3 medium beetroot
175g icing sugar, plus more
  for the purée, if needed
3 large pomegranates
the juice and zest of 1 lime
1 tbsp vanilla extract
  (or rose water)
500ml double cream

Mince pies

There's nothing like home-made mince pies. For authenticity, we want misshapen, some cooked slightly more than others, some bubbling up and out from under their lids. We want them made by the children or using Granny's recipe with the secret ingredient. But at the same time, for Christmas parties we want them to look elegant, topped with stars and a light snow of icing sugar.

This recipe works very well on both fronts, producing elegant home-made dainties. The pastry is crisp with a hint of cinnamon and the filling nicely cuts just the right sort of corners for this time of year when there's always a great list of stuff to be doing. It starts with a jar of ready-made mince-meat, but I've added a cooking apple, orange and lemon zest and some nuts to lighten and give a different texture. If you have mincemeat left over after using up all the pastry, it should keep in an airtight container in the fridge for a week or so. And if you're really pushed for time, you can use ready-made shortcrust pastry.

Feel free to experiment and add other ingredients — a splash of rum or brandy, a good spoonful of cooked cranberries to add colour and tartness or any other diced dried fruit, such as prunes and figs.

MAKES ABOUT 16 MEDIUM-SIZED OR 30-40 MINI MINCE PIES

Blend the flour, butter, sugar and cinnamon carefully in a food processor until the mixture forms a light and crumbly ball. You might need to add a few sprinkles of very cold water to get it to hold. Add the egg and pulse lightly to mix it in to the pastry. Take the pastry out of the processor, wrap in cling film and place it in the fridge while you mix the filling.

Empty the jar of mincemeat in to a bowl. Peel and coarsely grate the apple and stir it in. Add the orange and lemon zests and chopped nuts and give it all a good stir.

Heat the oven to 180°C/160°C fan/gas mark 4.

Remove the pastry from the fridge and roll it out on a floured board. Start by cutting out 12 discs and stars to go with them. Depending on the size of your cutter, you should find the pastry will make more than this.

Gently press the pastry discs in to bun or tart tin moulds, spoon 2-3 teaspoonfuls of mincemeat in to each one and top with a pastry star.

Bake for 15 minutes or until the stars are golden. Once cooked, remove from the tins and leave to cool on a wire tray. Serve warm, generously dusted with icing sugar.

FOR THE PASTRY
250g plain flour, sifted
150g butter
75g caster sugar
½ tsp ground cinnamon
1 large egg, beaten

FOR THE FILLING
410g jar of good-quality
  mincemeat
1 medium Bramley apple
the zest of half an orange
the zest of half a lemon
a small handful of almonds,
  toasted and finely chopped
a small handful of hazelnuts,
  toasted and finely chopped

TO SERVE
icing sugar, for dusting

The morning-after-the-night-before breakfast

Vegetarians often get a bit of a raw deal and so, when we were first devising the Bill's café menu, we decided to change all that and give them, instead, a very good deal. We set about creating a number of real bells-and-whistles vegetarian dishes, including breakfast. And, I have to say, it is a bit of a cracker. It definitely nods in the direction of the traditional British fry-up, but it's much more glamorous and, obviously, healthier.

What's good about this is not only is it an award-winning Bill's breakfast, much loved by many a Bill's customer, but also that, if you made mezze for the party the night before and you have some leftover humous and guacamole, you're virtually there already. 'Humous and guacamole for breakfast?' I hear you cry. Try them, they're good.

This breakfast also happens to be perfect for hangovers, so if you wake in need of some soul food in the shape of a very hearty breakfast, this will do the job.

Here, then, is a list of what to include. It's up to you how you put it all together. And whether you're feeling delicate or not, a good pot of tea and jug of orange juice on standby add to the comfort and joy.

SERVES 1

2 slices of good bread, toasted
1 large spoonful of humous
  (see recipe on page 279)
1 large spoonful of guacamole
  (see recipe on page 282)
2 poached eggs

2 tomato halves, lightly fried or roasted
2 or 3 large flat mushrooms, lightly
  coated in oil and grilled or roasted
a drizzle of sweet chilli sauce
a good grind or two of coarse black pepper
fresh basil leaves, to garnish

Food for lazy days

One of the best times of the year is that period between Christmas and New Year. All the rushing around and fuss are over, there's enough food in the house to last till some time in the spring and, if you're lucky and don't have to work, you can just plan each day as it comes. It's the closest we come to being in that holiday frame of mind without leaving home.

It's a time for family and friends, wintry walks, trips to the pub, black-and-white films and board games, lighting the fire and keeping it going all day. And the food we prepare and eat should all be a part of these few lazy, take-it-as-it-comes days. We want dishes we can prepare with very little fuss, that can sit on the hob or in the oven for a while, so we can walk or snooze, watch an old film or beat everyone at Monopoly.

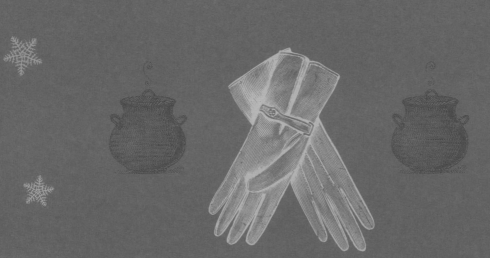

Thai butternut squash soup

First up – soup. Make the most of midwinter vegetables and add other textures and flavours to ring the changes: beans and lentils, tomato purée, dried oregano and a swirl of pesto for a taste of the Mediterranean; ginger, cumin and other spices for warming Indian soups; coconut milk and coriander for Thai-inspired bowls of comfort, like this smooth and soothing squash soup. This also works well using pumpkin instead.

SERVES 6

Heat a good splash of olive oil in a large, heavy-bottomed pan and gently cook the onions and celery for 10 minutes. Add the squash and potatoes and continue to cook on a low heat for another 15 minutes or so, keeping the lid on and stirring occasionally to prevent sticking.

Add the green curry paste, stir to coat the vegetables well and then pour in the vegetable stock.

Simmer for a further 15 minutes or so until the vegetables are soft, then add the coconut milk, half the chopped coriander and the honey. Stir, remove from the heat and allow to cool for a little while before blending thoroughly – it should be a really smooth, silky soup. Return to the pan and reheat to serving temperature.

Season to taste, and garnish each bowlful with a good pinch of the remaining chopped coriander.

olive oil
2 onions, diced
1 stick of celery, diced
1 large butternut squash,
  peeled and diced
2 large potatoes,
  peeled and diced
1 tbsp Thai green curry paste
1 litre hot vegetable stock
1 x 400ml tin of
  coconut milk
a large handful of fresh
  coriander, chopped
1 tbsp honey

Wintry beef and ale stew with cheese scones

Here's a dish for winter walk days: quick and easy to prepare, it sits in the oven for a couple of hours, can be doubled up to feed more if need be and it's even got crumbling cheese scones on top. Place some potatoes around the dish on the oven shelf to bake if you like or if you want the stew to stretch a bit further. Then steam some cabbage or broccoli just before you're ready to eat.

SERVES 6–8

Preheat the oven to 180°C/160°C fan/gas mark 4.

Heat a good splash of olive oil in a large casserole and gently cook the onion, carrot and celery for 10 minutes until soft, then add the garlic and cook for a further 2–3 minutes. Put the vegetables in a dish to one side, and cook the beef in the pan (in batches if necessary) for 5 minutes or so, until it is browned all over. Put the vegetables back in the pan with the beef and add the chopped tomato, stock and beer and bring to the boil. Season well with salt and freshly ground black pepper, put the lid on the casserole and place in the oven to cook for 1½–2 hours.

To make the scones, rub the flour, butter and baking powder together with a pinch of salt until breadcrumb-like, then stir in the cheese. Pour in enough milk to bind the mixture and combine to make a dough. Using a little flour, roll the dough in to walnut-sized balls and cover with a damp cloth until you are ready to add them to the stew. They need to sit on top for the last 30 minutes of cooking time, with the lid on for the first 15 minutes, then off so that they brown.

Serve each bowlful of steaming stew with a scone, a spoonful of mustard and a sprinkle of thyme on top.

olive oil
1 onion, diced
1 carrot, peeled and diced
4 sticks of celery, diced
2 garlic cloves, finely chopped
700g stewing beef, cubed
1 medium tomato, finely chopped
570ml beef stock
2 x 275ml bottles of porter or stout

FOR THE CHEESE SCONES
175g self-raising flour, sifted
50g butter, cut in small pieces
½ tsp baking powder
75g strong Cheddar, grated
50–60ml milk

TO SERVE
6 dsp wholegrain mustard
6 sprigs of fresh thyme

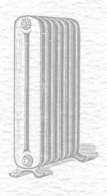

Sticky toffee pudding

And so we come to the last recipe in the book, and it could be argued that this being a book about following the seasons and encouraging us all to eat — for the most part — healthily from the best of what's in the garden or the shops, we should mark the moment with an appropriate recipe. But, no. I choose sticky toffee pudding. Brazenly unhealthy and no connection whatsoever to the seasons. Sometimes you just have to let it all go.

SERVES 6-8

Preheat the oven to 180°C/160°C fan/gas mark 4 and lightly butter and line a 23 x 23cm ovenproof dish or tin.

Place the dates in a bowl, pour 275ml of boiling water on top, add the baking soda and leave to soak for 10 minutes before blitzing the mixture in a food processor. If you don't have a food processor, mash the dates with a fork.

Meanwhile, whisk the sugar and eggs together in a large bowl until pale and creamy, stir in the melted butter, yoghurt and vanilla extract, and fold in the flour. Lastly, fold in the mashed dates, ensuring they are well distributed through the mixture.

Pour the sponge mixture in to the tin and bake for 20-25 minutes, until the top is firm and springy to the touch. Remove from the oven.

Preheat the grill while you make the toffee sauce. Place all the sauce ingredients in a pan and heat through until they have melted together. Pour a third of the sauce mixture over the sponge pudding and place it under the grill until the top is hot and bubbling.

Allow the pudding to cool slightly before serving with the remaining sauce in a jug, some good vanilla ice cream and a growing sense that if there's home-made sticky toffee pudding on the table, then at this very moment, all is right with the world.

Ah yes: cook, eat, smile.

180g whole stoned dates, chopped
1 rounded tsp baking soda
100g soft brown sugar
2 large eggs
90g unsalted butter, melted
2 tbsp thick plain yoghurt
1 tsp vanilla extract
175g self-raising flour, sifted

FOR THE TOFFEE SAUCE
250ml double cream
150g unsalted butter
100g muscovado sugar
50g molasses

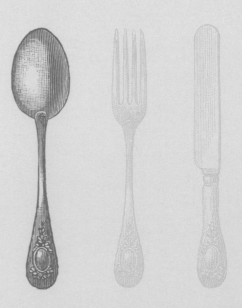

Lots of people have helped us to build this book.
Their inspiration, skills in the kitchen, recipe suggestions,
honest appraisals, frank exchanges, time, patience and endless
support have all contributed to giving our book wings.

So, huge thank yous go to the following people:

Everyone at Saltyard Books

Elizabeth, Al, Bryony, Leni, Cliff, Jo, Mandi and the rest of the team.

For photography, design, food styling and recipe testing

Dan Jones and Andrew Burton; Ami Smithson at Cabin London;
Katie Giovanni and Julia Azzarello.

The staff at Bill's, with honourable mentions for Fredi Djuric for cooking
and help with recipes; Lou Carter for her beautiful handwriting; Scott Buckle for
holding everything together; and to Bryan Parrott for taxi-ing us and produce all
over the place at a moment's notice.

David Bland at Flint Owl Bakery for his delicious bread.

Marcus Cload for sharing his pizza dough recipe.

Hannah for helping with a cake that was almost bigger than her.

Simon Walker for testing recipes.

Charlotte Faber for playing with the cherry spooning sauce until it was perfect.

Andy Pellegrino for the ideas, work and commitment he put into shaping Bill's.

Big thanks also to all the Bill's customers who either agreed to be in our
pictures or put up with us shooting around them.

And finally, of course, special thank yous to our families:

To Becca, for everything; to Tania for all her work with Bill's
and being the best big sister; to George, Alfie and Bertie for posing,
eating and generally being around the place. And to Robin, Peggy and Joe
for their support, good humour and for making endless cups of tea.

We could possibly have done it without you,
but it wouldn't have been so much fun.

cafe produce store cafe

Bill's

produce store cafe

food and drinks

bill's quick supper

now available in our brighton store

from sunday – friday 5pm – 7pm

a choice of main dishes at £6.95

Index

First published in Great Britain in 2011 by Saltyard Books
An imprint of Hodder & Stoughton
An Hachette UK company

2

Text © Bill Collison and Sheridan McCoid, 2011
Photography © Dan Jones, 2011

A CIP catalogue record for this title is available from the British Library.

ISBN 978 1 444 70390 0

Typeset in Mrs Eaves and Clarenden
Design by www.cabinlondon.co.uk
Managing editor Bryony Nowell
Copy editor Lesley Levene
Proof reader Margaret Gilbey
Indexer Caroline Wilding

Printed and bound in England by Butler, Tanner and Dennis Ltd

Hodder & Stoughton policy is to use papers that are natural, renewable and recyclable
products and made from wood grown in sustainable forests. The logging and manufacturing
processes are expected to conform to the environmental regulations of the country of origin.

Saltyard Books
338 Euston Road
London NW1 3BH

www.saltyardbooks.co.uk